DESIGN

BETWEEN THE LINES

PATRICK LE QUÉMENT

DESIGN
BETWEEN THE LINES

Foreword by
STEPHEN BAYLEY

With complementary texts by
STÉPHANE GEFFRAY

Illustrated by
GERNOT BRACHT

MERRELL
LONDON · NEW YORK
merrellpublishers.com

Contents

Foreword
Stephen Bayley

Proceeding down the road in a sequence of more-or-less controlled explosions, the car was the ultimate analogue experience. Behind the wheel, the driver felt enthroned – if not always in a good way.

And as we near the end of the era of the private car, it's becoming ever more clear that the great automobiles of the past were, along with rock music, ads and the movies, among the most singular achievements of our culture.

At the same time, the concept of 'designer' is losing its meaning, at least in the sense of an individual imposing his or her will on huge volumes of mass-produced goods. In our atomized, crowd-sourced, pixellated, diversified moment, no individual can any longer influence an entire industry.

So it follows that the great car designers were exceptional individuals. And Patrick le Quément was one of them. He was perhaps the most original designer working in the conservative car business at the turn of the millennium.

Patrick was at Ford for the introduction of the Cortina Mark IV, one of the most handsome cars of its genre and generation. And he was there when its successor, the Sierra, appeared. This last was among the most aesthetically radical cars to enter the mainstream.

Yes, after some public resistance to the Sierra's novelty, the air was rank with the aroma of burning fingers, but an emphatic point had been made: mass-market was no longer to be defined by dullness and complacency. Raymond Loewy, pioneer design consultant, said '*la laideur se vend mal*' (ugliness doesn't sell well). Patrick thought '*l'ennuyeux se vend mal*' (boring stuff doesn't sell well).

Renault gave Patrick his chance. To him, 'design' was as much a matter of thinking as a matter of drawing. Rather as Le Corbusier once noted, design is intelligence made visible.

It was in his early Renault years that Patrick and I got to know each other. I remember him picking me up at my Paris hotel in a Twingo. The novelty of the car astonished me: strange colours, interesting interior, indefinable gender. If we look now at a 1993 Twingo and think, 'so what?', it just proves how much Patrick's ideas about design have successfully influenced everyone else.

Then there was the Scénic, which I first saw as a model in the Paris studios: this was design not as tinkering with a radius, finessing a detail, but as a way of rethinking what personal transport should be. I bought one. With my own money. And, later, I acquired an Avantime; a supreme novelty, this was one of the most wonderful, imaginative and enjoyable cars ever. Alas, it was perhaps too imaginative for customers stuck on Bismarck-era notions of German prestige.

Happily, many of the long conversations Patrick and I enjoyed took place in very good restaurants, food and wine being shared passions. Design, you see, is rather like cooking. You need good ingredients, just as you need good materials. You need a recipe or a concept. Food must be nutritious, just as design must work well. And, of course, each must be delicious and delight the consumer.

No one is, I think, anticipating much delight in the cars of the future. But there is great pleasure to be found in the cars of the recent past. Meanwhile, Patrick le Quément has not changed, even if the world has.

Nowadays, he designs boats.

Introduction

When I began my career as an automotive designer, I felt compelled to shape the change rather than just change the shape; not an easy choice as it turned out, but then it could never have been otherwise. After all, I studied industrial design at what was then named the Birmingham College of Art and Design (now part of Birmingham City University), where I had the privilege of having as a professor Naum Slutzky, who had as a young man been a teacher at the most influential design school of the twentieth century, the Bauhaus in Weimar, Germany. One day, Herr Slutzky burst into a drawing class and asked us students to stop drawing the objects before our eyes and concentrate instead on drawing the spaces *between* the objects. It changed my life, as I learned to look at the world from various viewpoints. It is said that a mind that is stretched never returns to its original size. And that is how it came to be that I did not choose the most obvious theme to gain acceptance from the diploma jury; I chose to design a cyborg... and I did gain the jury's attention.

Perhaps this willingness to take calculated risks was due to my having lived through a character-forming youth, what with having been born in France, in Marseille, that wonderful sun-drenched and yet windy city where the mistral wind can chill your bones. My father was a car enthusiast and I have fond memories of being driven in some odd cars, such as a special-bodied Citroën Licorne and a Hudson Terraplane. He was also an officer in the French Foreign Legion whose family were pure Bretons (the people of Brittany), while my mother, a former nursing sister, was a rather rebellious Englishwoman from Lancashire. My father died in a freak accident accompanying a friend of the family who had won a Renault 4CV in a lottery and had managed to obtain her driving licence through my father's persistent encouragement, on her sixth attempt.

I do not want to sound callous, but his death transformed my life as suddenly, the following year I found myself in a preparatory school in London, the only French boy on earth. I learned to speak English and soon moved on from talking with a typically French accent to sounding like a native-born British boy, but my surname remained a giveaway; I could never, ever get anyone to pronounce it properly.

Later, many, many years later, that handicap still stuck to me until one day in London while I was head of Renault Design, I was invited to come up on stage to receive a prize and the announcer said: 'Ladies and gentlemen, the moment has now come to name the winner of this year's Designer of the Year Award, I invite Patrick Luckyman to come up on stage.' The name stuck as it reflected precisely what I had enjoyed so far in my career, working in so many different countries, meeting so many inspiring people within different companies such as Simca, Ford, Volkswagen-Audi and of course Renault.

I began in an industry in which design was called 'styling', and that is exactly what was asked of its members: namely, to superficially alter the appearance of vehicles that had ungainly proportions. Styling was an obscure activity whose members reported to Engineering and were treated like vassals who were seldom invited to participate in adult meetings. Stylists working in the automobile industry made up a very small group of individuals; in most companies they could be counted on the fingers of one hand, unlike today when there are hundreds of designers within a design department. But then, most of the creative input, from the 1960s all the way through to the 1980s, came from the highly talented Italian *carrozzerie* (coachbuilders).

This book reflects the formidable changes that occurred throughout those years, the shift in paradigm that took place when design replaced styling, when designers began to be looked upon as significant assets who could transform the destiny of a company.

The book is not an autobiography as such, but it does relate my individual journey through fifty years of thoughts, actions, failures and successes, and also comprises observations and comments about design, about some of those extraordinary brands that made up our shared cultural heritage. It is also about life generally and that remarkable contraption called 'the automobile', which so influenced the lives of millions of people the world over from the end of the nineteenth century right up to today. An independent observer once calculated that I had been responsible for some sixty million vehicles during my active career as an automotive designer, and this I feel makes me a legitimate commentator.

Design: Between the Lines is made up of fifty 'perspectives', essays that are sometimes autobiographical. They cover automobile history and refer to some brands of the past such as Voisin, to great architects like Le Corbusier, to the fundamentals of good design and the positioning of design within a modern organization. I speak of *concours d'élégance*, including the Villa d'Este where I have been a judge for more than two decades; of collectors and their collections; of the rise and sad fall of the Italian *carrozzeria*. I reminisce about the birth of that rascal of a car named Twingo, about the genesis of the Logan, about Bristol and Connolly (two glorious names of the past and yet still very much present). I discuss matters touching on concepts and culture, on the creative organization, on strategy and, of course, on management, be it of people or of brands. In fact, I have dwelled on all the subjects that were not included in my two biographies as these had to include so many other predetermined themes.

In Alexandre Dumas's historical adventure novel *The Three Musketeers* (1844), it turns out that they were in fact four, and so it is with those who actively participated in the crafting of this book. First there is Stéphane Geffray, a university academic, journalist and automobile afficionado who encouraged me to persevere and who wrote the very lively complementary and informative texts that accompany my perspectives. Then there is my sporting partner, Gernot Bracht, a great German design illustrator and teacher at the School of Design at Pforzheim University as well as at Austria's FH Joanneum University, who drew the quite remarkable illustrations within these pages, all of them concentrations of both expressivity and artistic finesse. Each of the drawings was the outcome of incessant exchanges that can be likened to an eighteen-month-long game of table tennis. Finally, there is Jean-Marie Souquet with whom I've worked for so many years at Renault, a rigorous sparring partner who continuously pushed me into the corner of the boxing ring in order for me to better qualify each single word, comma and nuance.

When I began to write this book, I did not have a final destination in mind. Continuous searching led to findings that made me understand where I wanted to go. I hope you will enjoy the ride.

1
Design and Drawing

People I meet often express surprise when I tell them that after I left my job as director of design at Renault, one of my first tasks – and by no means my easiest – was to learn how to draw again. The explanation is simple: my primary mission throughout the twenty-two years I spent at Renault, even more so than in my previous jobs at Volkswagen, Ford and Simca, was to inspire, to encourage and to provide direction to my teams of designers. By the time I left Renault, we had 140 designers. I had forbidden myself to so much as pick up a pencil because I felt it was more important to help others work better, and also because any proposals emanating from me could have been counterproductive. For – and let's be clear about this – whether they are good or bad, the boss's ideas are still the boss's ideas, and I didn't want anything of that nature to distort the design process.

So did this mean that I could no longer count myself a designer, just because I had stopped drawing? Far from it! It is not for nothing that the French language, along with others – including English, naturally – distinguishes *design* from *dessin* (drawing), as well as from *style*. Design encompasses a universe of skills. Right at the top of the list I would put the ability to conceive objects that fulfil their function as perfectly as possible, yet which can also be produced at the most affordable prices and to the highest feasible levels of quality. And when it comes to cars, these must lend themselves to being manufactured in large numbers. Or, to put it another way, you could draw a bird, but you would never be able to design one, as each bird is a unique living individual shaped by its own personal circumstances.

As for the distinction between design and style, that too is very clear: a particular object, perhaps impractical or even without a purpose, can be very beautiful thanks to its style. But in the world of design, and picking up on the 'form follows function' maxim of the late nineteenth-century American architect Louis Sullivan, beauty stems from how successfully an object achieves its purpose.

Design makes the clearest sense when it is applied to those objects for which the need is greatest at any given point in time. When the discipline of 'design' emerged at the end of the nineteenth century, it began by rethinking architecture and furnishing – just as urbanization was beginning to really take off. And after World War I, when cars became accessible to large numbers of people, design began to be applied to the automobile.

A perfect expression of the aspirations of an era would be a Voisin parked outside the Modernist Villa Savoye near Paris designed by Le Corbusier in 1928: a car of exemplary modernness and an elegant and well-appointed weekend residence. A quarter of a century before the 'Trente Glorieuses' post-World War II boom took hold in France, this pairing provided a glimpse of what was to become everybody's dream, whether that dream focused on the objects themselves or the prosperous lifestyles they promised.

But what about today? What lifestyle(s) are we dreaming of? What aspirations, and what promises? We are living in a world in which the virtual is increasingly present – to the point that, in the design of an object, it has become essential to encompass the design of its services. It is 'connected' objects that are now capturing the attention of designers: just as the Citroën DS was a design icon in the 1950s, the icon of the past ten years has been the iPhone. Does this mean that most people no longer define their desires in terms of an automobile? And that creative people of today and tomorrow will focus their talents in other arenas, away from cars? Myself, I would not go quite that far, even though right now a good deal of my design activity centres on boats.

Car design may have arrived at a crossroads, for it needs to change, just as cars themselves need to. A Ferrari from the 1960s, or on a more basic level a Ford Capri 2600 RS, spelt out a promise of freedom and individuality, of motorways that allowed you to

The Voisin C7 Lumineuse and Le Corbusier's Villa Savoye in Poissy, France.

Two icons of design:
the Citroën DS and
the iPhone.

cross Europe at up to 120 mph. That was true then, and at the time it was perfectly possible to imagine that this was just the beginning. Today, there are plenty of cars that still tell that story, even though it is no longer a story that people can subscribe to. Even a Tesla, although futuristic and remarkable in so many ways, picks up on the same ultraclassical design codes as a Maserati Quattroporte. But why does a breakthrough product such as the Tesla feel the need to align itself so closely with last century's identity? Surely there is a bold new vision of the future waiting to be conceived here?

Design and beauty for all

Who was the first designer? There is obviously no answer to that question. However, it is clear that the very idea of creating beautiful industrial products is intrinsically linked to industry, and more precisely to the Industrial Revolution in the late eighteenth century. Until then, craftsmanship had been the norm, and with it a variety that could be seen in the most mundane products. Traditional knives, which are so different from one country, one region, sometimes even one town to another, provide a striking example of this phenomenon. With the beginnings of mass production came a double challenge: manufacturers had to sell their mass-produced goods, or fail. Hence, these goods needed to be attractive, functional and affordable. For many thinkers of the nineteenth century, such as the English designer William Morris, the Industrial Revolution was a unique opportunity to bring beauty into the everyday life of the ever-growing working class. Design, in its modern meaning, came out of this necessity. And with it, came products that more than stood the test of time, such as the Austrian Thonet No. 14 chair (1859), the UK's Clifton Suspension Bridge (1864), and the American Zippo lighter (1933).

2

St Augustine's

In these Brexit-dominated times I keep harking back to the categorical 'Non!' of Charles de Gaulle in a memorable press conference on 14 January 1963: the French president was implacably opposed to the UK's entry into the Common Market, citing Britain's indissoluble bonds with America and the fact that the UK was so insular and so strongly British that it would never manage to fit in.

At the time I was just beginning my training as a designer at an English university, and I remember the 'anti-froggy' campaign waged by the popular press as being very real and pretty inflammatory. Earlier, I'd had to get used to their strange sense of humour vis-à-vis their cross-Channel neighbours: 'Wonderful country, France,' they would say, 'pity about the French.'

Fortunately, I had become hardened to British taunts as I had already been pursuing my studies for several years in that beautiful country. My mother had sent me to England after my father had died in an accident as he accompanied a novice driver taking her first go at the wheel. That is how, at the age of twelve, I found myself at Eddington House, a school in London, not knowing a word of English. I had been parachuted into a sect that sported garish, multicoloured uniforms that to me initially appeared to be verging on the ridiculous. And of course, the other pupils mocked me for being so different – and I laughed at them because they were all identical. Among the bizarre things they wore were three-quarter-length trousers that finished halfway down their calves; the trousers were so baggy that you had to take two or more steps before your extended shorts caught up with you.

After spending a year in London I was accepted by a so-called 'public school' at Ramsgate on the Kent coast: St Augustine's College. The pupils' parents were allowed to take their offspring out each weekend, and it was then that I first began to appreciate the archaic splendour of British cars – the high and mighty Rolls-Royces, the aristocratic

Bentleys, the exceptionally ugly Daimlers, beautiful old Jaguars, Armstrong Siddeleys from an era long since passed, and the occasional, rare, Bristol. Those who were less well off, or those forced to make the choice between investing in education for their children or taking pleasure in motoring, arrived in more modest machinery, sometimes quite elderly but always well maintained. I remember noticing the paintwork on a Wolseley 4/44, a firebrand if ever there was one, with its 0–60 mph in 30 seconds; the paint had been worn completely away in several areas thanks to regular polishings each weekend. And then there were others such as the Austin Atlantic, which resembled a beached whale, a caricature surpassed only by the tiny Austin A30 in the naivety of its styling: both looked as if they'd just been stamped out by the same cookie cutter.

Worst of all was the Triumph Mayflower, as stiff and upright as a butler at a formal London society occasion. The Mayflower's style gave the impression of something that had been shrunk to 7:8 scale – which is precisely the trick you find played by the buildings in the Walt Disney theme parks. Its every facet was shaved to the bone, to an extent that made it close to being a stealth aircraft before its time. If there had been a pan-European contest for ugliness in those days, the Mayflower might have been elevated to the top step of the podium, or maybe the second... along with the Daimler Dart, or SP250. Just mentioning that name gives me goose flesh.

Barely three years into its life, the Dart found itself confronted with the Jaguar E-Type. One of my British designer friends recounts the story of how as a very young visitor to the London motor show he found the Jaguar stand so crammed with people that it was almost impossible to get near to the star of the show. Being small, he was able to wriggle his way through the crowds to see the wondrous machine up close. His next objective

Left to right: The Austin A30, the Wolseley 4/44 and the Triumph Mayflower.

was to check out the Daimler Dart; there was not a single visitor on that stand, just a solitary salesman seated behind a table. In all likelihood the man was at the end of his tether and at that very moment applying for a job in Jaguar's sales department, disillusioned by all the criticisms he had read and heard about the ghastly monster he was representing. He did not even give my friend the chance to ask for a brochure: 'Clear off!' he grumbled. 'I've got other things to do.' To which my friend retorted, 'I see, so it's that serious!', and made off without waiting for the salesman's reply.

This was in the 1960s, when the British auto industry had chosen to lead its life cut off from a European continent that seemed distant and, frankly, alien in character. No people were more alien than we French, who already had a reputation among the British for making cars that were strange in both their design and how they drove. For the British the Citroën 2CV epitomized the French malaise, closely followed by Citroën's Ami 6 and, at quite some distance, the Renault 4. This, it was conceded, was at least quite practical, even if it was lightweight in the quality of its construction. Looking back on this era, the principal thought that occurs to me is that it is sometimes a good idea to get out and about – as encapsulated elegantly in an Indian saying: 'The world is dark when you close your eyes.'

A poisonous dart

At first sight, designing and producing a car do not seem to bear any relation to tragedy. Yet some cars seem to have been born under a bad sign and bound to fail from the very start. Sometimes, as with the Tucker Torpedo of 1948, economics and politics conspire; sometimes, as with the French Facellia of 1959, an overlooked weakness (in this case, the engine) can lead to disaster. And then sometimes fate strikes through inexplicably bad design, as was the case with the Daimler Dart (also 1959). Technically speaking, the Dart had many qualities: its fibreglass body was innovative, and so were its disc brakes; Daimler, in spite of the antics of chairman Sir Bernard Docker and his wife, Lady Docker, remained the oldest British marque; last but not least, the car featured a wonderful 2.5 litre V8 engine designed by Edward Turner, of Triumph and BSA fame. Alas, there was its tortured design, its gaping mouth, and also a chassis so flexible that doors sometimes opened during spirited driving. The Dart disappeared in 1964, and precipitated Jaguar's takeover of Daimler. Only its engine would survive for a short time, in the Daimler version of Jaguar's Mark 2 saloon, and soon Daimlers were merely high-end versions of Jaguars, until 2007 when Jaguar stopped using the Daimler nameplate.

3

Bristol and Connolly

Our magnetic attraction to the smell of leather: where does it come from? Does it hark back to our earliest days, when Homo sapiens protected themselves from the elements by wrapping up in the skins of the animals they had hunted? Or could it be that, as suggested by Jean-Claude Ellena, the former *parfumier* at Hermès, 'the very best leathers smell of flowers' and thus bring to mind nature and everything that is authentic?

Leather was considered to be a noble material as long ago as in ancient Egypt, and was used for fashioning garments and accessories. For my part, I first began drawing in deep lungfuls of the smell of leather in the Bristol belonging to my mother's friends who would pick me up from the Gare de Lyon in Paris when I arrived off the train from Marseille. I would normally stay with them in Aubervilliers, just outside the capital, for two days before being put onto another train, leaving from the Gare du Nord this time, to Dieppe. After the Channel crossing to Newhaven I would board the quintessentially English train to London, its carriages reeking strongly of coal and their interiors upholstered in rough velour. The merest thought of that journey via Waterloo station before each school term was enough to make me prickle with rage: 'Welcome to Great Britain, Frenchy!'

Back, however, to Bristols. Just to be clear, these sporting cars were highly individualistic: they were handmade and Bristol's aeronautical expertise showed through in every aspect of their design, even though the company itself had a somewhat troubled history that meant it could move ahead only at a sloth-like pace. The Bristol that belonged to our kind friends (he a doctor with a distinguished record of service and she an English Lady) was kept alongside the family's two other cars in a garage and reflected the rather traditional taste of the mistress of the house. She herself drove an MG Magnette and their son, who had also studied in England, enjoyed a delectable MGA roadster to cover the miles and capture everyone's hearts; it was finished in a sublime cherry red, paired with a special interior trimmed in Connolly leather, just like the Bristol. I have especially strong memories of a trip to the Sologne area, near Orléans, where our friend was invited to join a hunting party. This gave me time for a close-up appreciation of the other prestigious cars that had arrived for the occasion: among them were two beautiful Maseratis, a very rare Aston Martin DB Mark III, and also a splendid Ford Comète, a model that to this day remains underrated.

Thinking of those two names, Bristol and Connolly, is enough to transport me back to another world, a bygone era that, even though India and Pakistan had been granted their independence back in 1947, still seemed everlasting in the 1950s. This world, the world of the British Empire, might have been losing its lustre but it still held a powerful and appealing fascination, conjuring up images of village cricket matches, Pimm's No.1, straw boaters or even Worcestershire sauce, that famous sweet-and-sour condiment invented in 1837 and most definitely the preserve of native English people.

I am lucky enough to count among my friends Anthony Hussey, the son of one of the Connolly daughters. He was marketing director of the Connolly family business, which dated back to 1878 but which, tragically, had to go into liquidation in 2002 as the result of an unwise decision to uproot its original workshop from Wimbledon and set up shop in Ashford, Kent. (The brand has since been resurrected, albeit as a very different operation.) The move lost the company most of its highly skilled craftsmen, artisans who were irreplaceable and who, as Anthony told me, represented centuries of expertise and experience. The whole premise of the move had been to improve the productivity of the workshops and to allow Connolly to extend its range downwards. The bankruptcy came as a huge blow to all classic-car enthusiasts, too: losing Connolly meant not only the loss of its unique set of skills but also that of its whole heritage as a supplier to

The Bristol 405.

the world's most prestigious manufacturers, such as Rolls-Royce, Bentley, Aston Martin, Jaguar and Ferrari. Even the very first signature armchair that Ludwig Mies van der Rohe designed for the 1929 Barcelona World Fair was trimmed in Connolly leather, and so, too, were the seats in the Concorde supersonic airliner. Anthony also worked with my dear friend Andrée Putman, who sadly died in 2013; she was a noted interior architect, celebrated as the diva of French design, and her collaboration with Anthony resulted in the magnificent Connolly flagship store opened in London in 1995.

Yet today, when I think of Bristols it is my friend Stefano Pasini who comes to mind. An ophthalmologist of worldwide repute, he is also the author of numerous books on automobile models and marques, among them Bristol. That's not entirely coincidental as he owns two examples, a 403 and a 409. An enthusiast with true passion, he has been involved in the Villa d'Este *concorso d'eleganza* for many years as a fellow jury member (see page 192). At the most recent competition I took the opportunity of settling myself into the cockpit of Stefano's 1954 Bristol 403. I immediately picked up on that very British feel – the burr walnut dashboard, the random scattering of controls and switches that give the impression they could have been picked from the spare-parts shelves at Retromobile. But what charm, what serenity flowed from that cabin! And what about that subtle smell of Connolly leather? In the space of just a few instants, it had transported me into the past, back into an era when my English classmates and I were in shorts that were too long and too baggy. That smell is my equivalent of Marcel Proust's madeleine biscuit, if you like…

Simply different

For the nineteenth-century British philosopher and economist John Stuart Mill, 'the amount of eccentricity in a society has generally been proportional to the amount of genius, mental vigour and moral courage which it contained.' By this standard, Bristol cars said much about Great Britain: born after World War II from the Bristol Aeroplane Company, the automaker had fairly normal beginnings: its first car, the 400, was almost a clone of the pre-war BMW 326, 327 and 328. Still, very quickly, Bristol cars started to be different, following principles that, for company founder Sir George White, were more important than fashion: ergonomics had to be first-class; aerodynamics were a priority (the 1949 401 reached 100 mph with only 85 bhp); cars had to be narrow for manoeuvrability; and the 1953 404 located the spare wheel and battery in the front wing to free up luggage space. Quirkier still was Bristol's commercial policy: exports never were a priority (although French president Georges Pompidou was a Bristol owner), and, after the former racing driver Tony Crook took over the company in 1973, Bristols were sold uniquely from the Kensington High Street dealership in London. Tony Crook himself decided if the potential customer was worthy of owning a Bristol.

4

Mad Dogs and Englishmen...

It was in 1930 that the English playwright Noël Coward wrote the song 'Mad dogs and Englishmen', the punchline of which is '...go out in the midday sun'. Who else but someone steeped in that uniquely British tradition of eccentricity could have come up with such offbeat humour – a total wackiness later turned up to the power of 10 by the Monty Python group or, more recently, by Rowan Atkinson as Mr Bean.

What's certain is that the English are truly something different, and that's why I love them so much. I love that sense of humour, something that energizes them and which crops up in some of the most unexpected and most dramatic situations. Who else, do you imagine, could have had such a sense of the ridiculous as to launch a product like the Reliant Robin, and then to crown the top-of-the-line version 'Royale'? And, anyway, who but the Brits could have dreamed up the name of a red-breasted garden bird for a car, especially one with just three wheels (one at the front, two at the rear)? This tiny saloon, launched in the 1970s, and later a van, were so bizarre that they soon came to be mocked as 'plastic pigs' on account of their glass fibre body shells. You don't have to look too far to realize that Britain is a nation of eccentrics – wacky people, as they would themselves concede. How else would you explain the fact that people in Britain buy more convertibles than those of any other country, even though the UK's verdant pastureland is a result of weather patterns guaranteed to keep frogs happy, but which is much less popular among the thousands of 'froggies' – or French expats – who have set up home there.

Evidence, too, is provided by the marvellous Morgan 3, another three-wheeler but this time with the two wheels where they are normally expected to be: in the front. This was the car that launched the Morgan marque in 1909 and was produced in the company's Malvern workshops through to 1952. A modern interpretation was unveiled at the 2011 Geneva motor show, powered by a Harley-Davidson engine and addressing the drawbacks of the original. The Morgan factory – or, more correctly speaking, the Morgan workshops – still occupies the same site close to the rolling green hills in the county of Worcestershire, right where the composer Edward Elgar drew inspiration for his music, in particular his captivating Violin Concerto in B minor of 1910. For my part I had the pleasure of driving a Triumph TR3 – hood firmly down, even when it was raining – through the narrow and winding lanes of the Malvern Hills. You do really have to ask yourself why the British buy so many convertibles when it rains so much there. And besides, whenever the conversation turns to cabriolets it's England that immediately springs to mind: those lovely little British sports cars, the cricket, the warm beer. So, why do the British stand out from the crowd just when you least expect them to?

This is likely to have been the question of those who, from their vantage point on mainland Europe, used to turn a Nelsonian blind eye towards creations emanating from the 'perfidious Albion'. For decades, European car manufacturers had stopped looking at what was coming out of Britain as there had been so little technical innovation – until, suddenly in 1959, out of nowhere came a new and revolutionary concept, an innovation that would turn the global auto industry upside down. This was the Morris Mini Minor, later shortened to just Mini (see page 117), dreamed up by a brilliant British-Greek (though Turkish-born) engineer by the name of Alec Issigonis. Sir Alec, as he became in 1969, actually came across as more British than the native-born British themselves, convincing proof that the environment in which people live can have a decisive influence on their behaviour, their creativity and their tastes. There's a parallel with Ettore Bugatti: born in Italy in 1881, he set up shop in France to create cars that were not only light in weight but also of unrivalled intelligence in their design. So much so that all Bugatti's creations have come to symbolize the French spirit unique to that country's greatest engineers (see page 113).

It saddens me, however, that the flashes of genius I witnessed in the England of my youth

The Triumph TR3, hood down in typical British weather.

The 1970s Reliant
Robin (far right),
among the symbols
of Britain.

have by now given way to standardization on a global level. The more fortunate of the British now drive around in BMWs and their daily diet includes sushi and tuna snacks. The UK draws influences from all around, and nowadays it is getting harder and harder to eat badly there. No more fish and chips wrapped in yesterday's newspapers, which was the norm when I was a boy, when people would quip that printer's ink should be consumed only in moderation. Luckily though, England still has its people...

One person I remember with particular affection is Charles, a colour and trim designer who started his career at the same time as me at Ford of Britain. With his blond hair he looked just like the singer Art Garfunkel of the celebrated American duo Simon and Garfunkel. Yet Charles was in no way California cool when it came to his choice of clothes: his style showed a strong dominance of green, his tie was always knotted around his neck, and because of his aversion to fluorescent lighting he had to protect himself, just like American office workers from the previous century, with a transparent celluloid visor, also tinted green. This must surely have influenced his recommendations for Ford colour palettes, especially as, worryingly, his boss at the time, Non Crook, suffered from colour blindness – hardly an asset in his line of work.

During the course of my career I have worked in a great number of studios in Europe – in Germany, in the UK, in Spain, in Italy and in Central Europe; I've also worked in the United States, in South America, in Asia and even in Australia. Of course all these studios had a lot of qualities in common, but there were two things that made the British studio where I worked very different from the rest. It was the only studio I have ever been in where there was a continuous soundtrack in the background, where you could hear people singing and, interspersed at regular intervals, wild explosions of laughter. And it was also the only one in my career where I was able to witness a band made up of modellers, technicians and designers making music in their lunch hour – and chewing through Spam and pickled onion sandwiches at the same time. One thing is for sure: these English always like to do things differently!

Mad dogs, or...?

'Great Britain is an island, wholly encircled by waters': thus began the lectures on the United Kingdom given by the French sociologist André Siegfried to his students in the early twentieth century. Useless truism? Maybe, but then again, maybe not. For the British, being islanders is part of their identity, so much so that Shakespeare's Richard II celebrates 'This royal throne of kings, this scepter'd isle, this earth of majesty...' Britain's insularity has also played a part in the country's automotive culture: paradoxically, the nation that invented free trade did for a long time protect its industry with heavy import duties, to the extent that, in 1968, a 1.8 litre, 115 hp Alfa Romeo 1750 cost as much as a 4.2 litre, 265 hp E-Type Jaguar. This situation often led to products that were specifically designed for the home markets, and, unfortunately, did not contribute to profitability, as the sad history of British Leyland in the 1970s shows. From Armstrong Siddeleys to Lanchesters, from Bristols to Marcoses, the A-Z of British cars can often be read as a quirky catalogue of idiosyncracies, especially for continental Europeans and Americans who rarely had a chance of spotting one on their home turf.

5

Coming to the Point

When I received my degree after four years studying industrial design, I already knew that I wanted to be a car designer – even though I had kept that quiet from my tutor, Naum Slutzky, who at the age of twenty-three had begun teaching at the legendary 1920s German design school, the Bauhaus (see page 89). For Slutzky, style represented a form of decadence, and foremost among the figures he hated was Raymond Loewy, the Franco-American who had risen to become one of the greatest stylists in the USA. The Shell logo that we know today was his work, as was the elegant 1953 Studebaker Starliner.

In 1952 Loewy opened up a subsidiary in Paris, which went by the name of Compagnie d'Esthétique Industrielle (CEI), or the Industrial Aesthetics Corporation. Once, when I was in Paris en route to the South of France, I stayed with family friends for a couple of days and they had the excellent idea of organizing a reception at which Raymond Loewy would be present. Implausible and incredible though it may seem, I don't remember anything about my conversation with him, although he did give me his business card with a view to fixing up a meeting later on. I have to confess that my attention had been focused elsewhere: in the direction of a very pretty young woman with whom I was engaged in a deep dialogue. I realized during the course of the evening that she had not fully understood what it was that I did in life: for her, an industrial aesthetician – the phrase that was in vogue in France at the time – seemed to be one of those new professions like conveyor-belt hairdressing salons.

I did go for an interview at CEI but the salary they offered me would have forced me into an uncomfortable choice: either to feed myself, or to pay the rent. That's how I came to join Simca, where the styling department was run by Claude Genest, who had earlier worked as a designer at General Motors (GM). His wardrobe reflected the time he had spent in Detroit; he wore trousers that were too short, revealing his splendid, though gigantic, shoes.

At that time, Simca was like an incubator for design talent. Robert Opron, for example, went on to join Flaminio Bertoni, the father of the Citroën DS and Ami 6; later, Opron would take over the reins of Style Citroën (see page 53). Simca's styling department was minuscule compared to a modern-day design division, which can number up to 500 people. When I joined, Simca design boasted a staff of just twenty-five, of whom three were interior stylists, with a similar number engaged on exteriors; three worked as full-scale draughtsmen, and there were modellers, two of whom were also involved in generating design proposals. Other individuals included a certain Jacques Nocher, a great character who had once been a talented boxer. A product of the Beaux-Arts art school, he found his expression in sculpture and in the evenings worked for Matra cars, where he designed the M530, a 2+2-seater coupé engineered by a brilliant team under Philippe Guédon.

One of the three exterior designers at Simca was John Pinko, an American who was a veteran of both Ford and Chrysler studios. He was an absolute ace at drawing and working with gouache, and could produce hyper-realist paintings in record time. Whenever there wasn't much work to do, I spent my time with him to learn all the latest drawing techniques practised in the American design centres. I progressed a long way, and quickly, too – and that is how I came to be transferred to exterior styling just three months after I had arrived.

As things turned out, I stayed only ten months at Simca: John Pinko and I had decided to leave and set up our own agency, Style International, to honour post-Bauhaus design movements and also Le Corbusier's Esprit Nouveau initiative. Our first move was to offer our services to the head of Simca, which at the time was owned by the American automaker Chrysler and had just named a new CEO, Harry Cheesbrough, whom John Pinko knew well. It was thanks to their shared

Raymond Loewy, his logo for the Lucky Strike cigarette packet and his 1953 Studebaker Starliner (top); students protesting in Paris in May 1968.

history that we were commissioned to design a replacement for the Simca 1000. Scoop photos of the prototype were published in *Paris Match* magazine two years later, but in the end this so-called mystery car was never built as Simca's model ranges were merged with those of the British Rootes Group, which had also been bought by Chrysler.

Other car design projects we were involved in included the Sovam 1300-GS, though our input was called for only very late in the programme, when its promoters were struggling to finalize the design.

The events in France of May 1968 and the political instability that followed meant the end of Style International: all our programmes were immediately cancelled. I straight away set about finding a job, and as all the French manufacturers had frozen their recruitment I turned towards Germany and, as a first priority, the European subsidiaries of GM and Ford. Ford was the first to reply, but during the interview I discovered that the job vacancy was not in Germany but in the UK, at the Ford Technical Centre in Essex. It seemed that some fifteen designers had just left to join the design centre of the newly formed British Leyland group. Having already spent some nine years in England for my education, I had hoped to explore new horizons. Nevertheless, I decided to accept the UK offer, in the full knowledge that the vacancy was in interior design. At the time this seemed to me to be a double blow, but later it was to prove a very important trump card. The practice of interior design is a separate discipline in its own right, and no one can put themselves forward for a management position without across-the-board experience. How lucky I was to have completed the toughest task right at the start.

Design vs architecture

Raymond Loewy's work in the mid-twentieth century is well documented and acknowledged, if only because of his shrewd sense of advertising. Indeed, his talents as a designer were crucial in the success of such icons as the Coldspot refrigerator and the Lucky Strike cigarette logo, and his work for Studebaker probably helped the car brand survive much longer than expected. However, his vision relied heavily on eye-catching features; as such, it found its absolute opposite in the work of his near contemporary, the architect and designer Charles-Edouard Jeanneret, better known as Le Corbusier. For Le Corbusier, only function was interesting, and embellishments were a despicable indulgence. As an architect, he applied these principles to his entire body of work, whether it was luxurious villas such as the Villa Savoye outside Paris, social housing schemes such as the Cité Radieuse in Marseille, or even churches. Le Corbusier's quest for absolute rationality even led him to conceive a whole development plan for Paris, in which the centre of the French capital was replaced by symmetrical skyscrapers linked by motorways. Cars and speed were so essential to his work that he designed a 'voiture minimum' in 1936. However, it was never built. Instead, 'Corbu' favoured the much more luxurious creations of his friend Gabriel Voisin, and, later, a Jaguar XK120.

6

Motown Memories

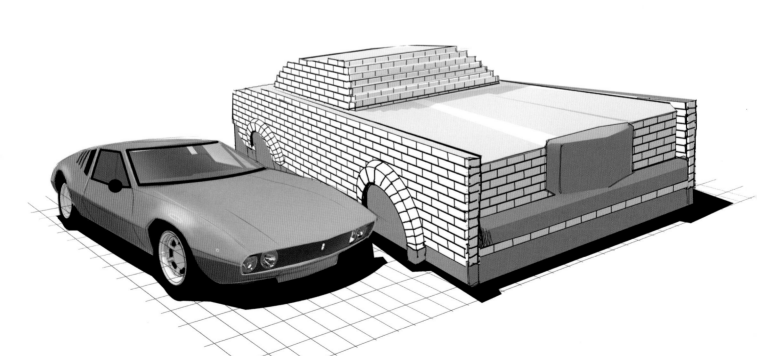

My first impression of Detroit was when I found myself in an outsize entry hall with a decor that immediately made me think of the decline and fall of the Roman Empire. Next was a succession of corridors, each as wide as a motorway; then there were rows of paint booths, followed by an immense studio. And at last, at the very far end, Ford's Exterior Design workshop. It was there that I needed to go to repair the scratches that the Corcel II styling model had suffered in transit between Europe and Detroit; the Corcel was a model aimed at the Brazilian market.

The workshop in question was supersize, too, and added to this was a pungent, all-pervading smell: the special clay used for sculpting the styling models, which gave off solvent vapours so acrid that I felt they were grabbing me by the throat. But what really made me rub my eyes in disbelief was the sheer number of models being worked on. No fewer than ten styling models were lined up in that workshop, each surrounded by a swarm of modellers in grey overalls, all of them lost in their own world but also forced to endure the sort of background muzak that could so easily have prompted me to switch professions.

Next to each model stood the designers, in three-piece suits the trousers of which seemed to my European eyes to be at least eight centimetres too short. This had the effect of highlighting the designers' disproportionately large shoes, many of them embellished with one or several chrome-plated details.

It was 1976 and this was my first business trip to the United States. It proved to be the starting point of a long story, a story that began two days later with a presentation to the company's CEO and chairman, Henry Ford II, grandson of the founder, and which ended nine years later with my resignation and my return, once and for all, to Europe.

Detroit, capital city of the American automobile, is often referred to as Motown (motor town). The city and its surroundings are given over to the development and production of cars, SUVs, pickups and trucks in their thousands or even their millions. If I had not resigned, this city would have been the permanent home for me and my family, for ever. It should be said that over the course of the years Detroit has degenerated into a metropolis pervaded by a latent violence that, sadly, became all too real while we lived there. The biggest fear expressed by most people was of breaking down late at night on the motorway, Interstate 94, that crosses the city: for many years the city could not afford to fix its street lights. Almost everywhere, shadowy figures would lurk menacingly around shops with windows – if they still existed – protected by steel shutters.

I have often asked myself whether the dramatic improvement in the reliability of American cars in the mid-1980s was connected to automakers' desire to match the performance of the Japanese in that regard, and thus remain competitive in the domestic market, or whether they quite simply wanted to get from one side of the city to the other without getting into trouble.

Despite all this I still treasure some excellent memories of Detroit: for example, family trips to the Henry Ford Museum of American Innovation, one of the most stimulating museums that I have visited. Its collections encompass not just cars but also steam trains and agricultural machinery exemplifying the lifestyles and the customs of this young country, all set against period backgrounds that only Walt Disney World could match.

And then there were the design centres I was able to visit – Ford, of course, but also GM's, which employed more than 1000 people. These were on an entirely different scale from European studios, where the volume of work was lower and the staffing levels more modest. By way of illustration, the number of new projects taken on by Detroit studios in the mid-1970s was matched in Europe only by the beginning of the 2000s. The Big Three (Ford, GM and Chrysler) had such vast resources that we, as Europeans, were made to feel

The De Tomaso Mangusta (far left) and the Lincoln Continental Town Car.

underdeveloped. But now, several decades later, we are seeing the flip side of that coin: in order to survive in the race it is the Americans who have had to begin studying the efficiency of Japanese and European design centres.

What also struck me was the sheer momentousness of some of the decisions being taken, as well as the far-sightedness of many Americans when it came to the challenge of boosting efficiency through digitization. In the very early 1980s Ford inaugurated its Studio 2000, tasked with bringing car design into the digital era through massive investments that blended talent with technology. But in 1997, when Ford's new director of design took up his post, he decided that digital technology had no place in design. 'Not sensitive enough', he proclaimed, which prompted the retort 'not yet' from the defenders of digital. Everything was dropped and as a consequence Ford Design went from being a pioneer, with at least a ten-year lead over its competitors, to being the dunce at the back of the classroom.

And then there were the delicious excesses of the bosses in the mid 1970s. For example, parked outside the executive offices, the two De Tomaso Mangustas purchased by Ford Design, the orange one for design vice-president Eugene Bordinat Jr and the metallic grey one for his deputy, Don DeLaRossa. But how could anyone drive a Mangusta and propose designs like the Lincoln Mark III decorated by the couturier Bill Blass?

One final recollection takes me back to an evening in 1976 when we were invited by Henry Ford II himself to dinner at head office to celebrate the success of the Brazilian project. As we reached the top floor he was there in person to welcome us at the lift doors. I remember my shock at the incredible thickness of the carpets, which gave the impression of walking on freshly fallen snow. A Château Margaux, Henry Ford's favourite wine, was served to the guests. That nectar straight away became emblematic for me and has remained so ever since – as has the Mangusta coupé.

The land rules

Henry Ford II's favourite wine was Château Margaux, an exceptional *grand cru classé* that epitomizes the character of the soil where it is grown, and which, as such, could not be reproduced anywhere else. In a way, automotive design is also the product of its geography. The wide open spaces of the USA may have been the source of a culture in which bigger has often meant better, and sometimes still does. Indeed, the proportions of American cars, especially before World War II, were much more balanced than those of their European counterparts, because their size was not an issue. However, size was not the only idiosyncrasy of American cars, which, for a very long time, also reflected two paradoxical sides of the American psyche. On the one hand there is a rather puritan restraint, deeply embedded in rural life, as exemplified by Henry Ford I's views on style, but also by the sobriety of such design landmarks as the first Lincoln Continental (1939). On the other hand there is a taste for ostentation which, post-war, was no longer the preserve of the richest and became available to all: colour-coded interiors, fins, vinyl roofs with opera windows, *faux bois* appliqués, all imagined by designers who were often larger than life themselves.

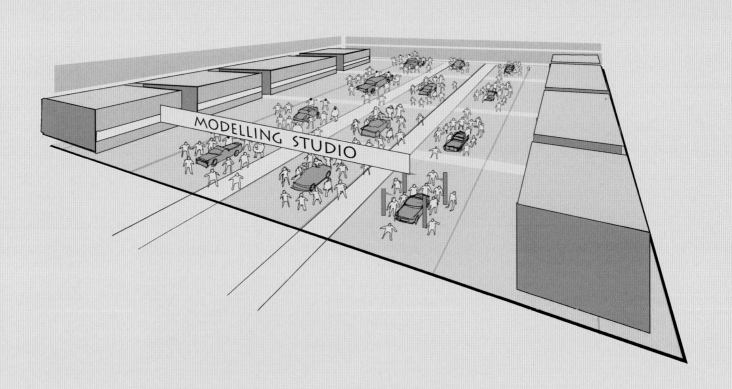

7

Stateside Recollections

'Time flew by while my back was turned', sang the Franco-Italian actor and singer Serge Reggiani in 1971, and these lines came back to me a few summers ago on a Michigan road when I spotted a 1987 Ford Thunderbird. It immediately took me back to that morning, many moons ago, when I arrived at the Ford Design Center in the Detroit suburb of Dearborn. It was June 1985 and I was starting a two-year posting to prepare myself for the role of vice-president of design for Ford of Europe; I was to replace the great Uwe Bahnsen, who was about to retire and who had named me as his successor.

The office allocated to me was still full of the odds and ends left by the man I was temporarily replacing, an American designer I had met a few years earlier at the Ford of Britain design centre when he came on a mission to pass on his immense talent to those in the Old World. As an illustrator, this young man had genius at his fingertips, but we did not share the same sense of good taste in automobile design.

Among his belongings were a lot of books and models and, most tellingly, a portrait of the current head of the design operation, positioned so as to catch the eye of anyone coming into his office. This gave me an instant insight into the gulf that existed between our two worlds. I immediately turned the portrait to face the wall, anxious that people might think it was mine and that in such a short space of time I had already succumbed to the local convention of unashamed five-star sycophancy. I remember being present when, in conversation with the newly appointed head of Ford Design, one of the design directors said: 'That's another stunning tie you're wearing – you've got truly remarkable taste!' I blushed on his behalf.

Outside my office, behind a large glass partition, sat the final, feasible models of the Ford Thunderbird and its sister car, the Mercury Cougar, which were to be launched in 1987. The project had recently been completed and they were due to go off into storage. Further to the left were fullsize clays of the cars that were going to replace them: the Tempo and Topaz had both just been approved, and they were going to fall within my area of responsibility. These two models represented the lowest low point of Ford design since the Edsel – not to mention the 1974 Mustang II: this was based on the Pinto, itself a response to the fuel crisis of 1973, and was about as attractive as a cheese grater. I completely failed to understand how a world-class design centre that had produced such legendary models as the Shelby Mustang and the 1961 Lincoln Continental could come up with a design as misshapen as the Mustang II, where every square inch of its surface gave the impression of having been shaped out of chewing gum.

The explanation lay in the fact that American design had been caught off guard by the fuel crisis and the need for a drastic reduction in the size of US cars. The response of studios was to make their designs much smaller, but to continue to include the features they were accustomed to from the enormous barges of the past, designs that many felt were true masterpieces. Their answer was to compensate for the lack of bulk by adding yet more strips of chrome and decorative embellishments; a Wurlitzer jukebox would seem like a puritan's handiwork by comparison.

But that was not all. In the wake of the fuel crisis came schemes to reduce the number of employees: underperformers were shown the door, along with those who were the most rebellious and, frequently, the most talented; plus there were all those excesses we Europeans had noticed on a daily basis, starting with the groupies who followed the boss around and fed him with compliments that became more and more disproportionate as time wore on. Sadly, the programmes launched around the mid-1980s reflected that climate of self-indulgence, something that put me in mind of this quotation from the 1987 Nobel Prize in Literature laureate, Joseph Brodsky: 'Aesthetics is the mother of ethics.' It should be noted that it was during this period

The Ford Lincoln Continental (far left) and the Ford Topaz.

Patrick le Quément
(in silhouette),
facing Jean-
François Venet
(centre) and
Michel Jardin on
a cruise down the
Mississippi river.

that the most monstrous body designs in the entire history of the automobile were penned by the Big Three, and that for a while they became veritable dwarves in the global art of automobile creativity.

Seated at my desk at the end of that day, 1 June 1985, it suddenly dawned on me that I could not subject myself to this visual pollution for two more years. So in spite of the fabulous promotion that had been dangled in front of me, I took the decision to go for a change of scene at the next available opportunity. Two months later I handed in my resignation as I had accepted an offer from the Volkswagen-Audi group. As there wasn't much to do in the studio in the intervening time, I took up an invitation to represent Ford Design at an international conference organized by a large American supplier based in Saint Paul, Minnesota. It was there that I met and immediately clicked with two senior executives from Style Renault, Michel Jardin and Jean-François Venet, who had also come as representatives of their organization. Two years down the line, when Gaston Juchet, head of Style Renault, decided to retire and a brilliant engineer emerged as the candidate to replace him, the genuine designers were anxious about seeing a non-designer in charge of the design centre: so much so that they threatened to go on strike. That was the trigger for the meeting called by Aimé Jardon, head of product development and overall number two at Renault, at which my name was put forward (see page 77). Was it luck or destiny? Maybe a bit of both...

Making decisions

Corporations, companies, administrations, governments are created and ruled by people. This means that, whatever they pretend, they are ruled by primary human emotions: lust, hubris, envy and fear. The latter can have dramatic consequences, not least where automotive design is concerned. Who indeed, if not motivated by sheer obsequiousness or pure fear, or both, could have thought that taking a decent Opel Ascona/Vauxhall Cavalier and dressing it up with a comprehensive catalogue of ritzy add-ons, such as swathes of chrome and duo-tone painting, would turn it into a real Cadillac (or, more precisely, into a 'Cimarron by Cadillac')? Or that branding a Dodge Omni as 'Shelby' would conjure up ghosts of Shelby Cobras past? Such blunders, of course, are not limited to the United States: when, a few years ago, Renault tried to resurrect the Gordini badge the failure was instantaneous, because the company forgot that the name had long stood for radical sportiness. The strange ideas of rebadging an old Oldsmobile Bravada as a Saab, a Nissan Cherry as an Alfa Romeo (albeit after fitting a true Alfa engine), and a Chrysler as a Lancia Flavia met the same fate. Deservedly.

8

Ketchup and Pomodori

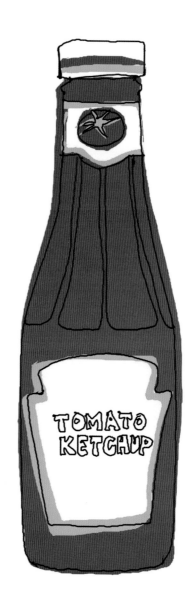

Joe Oros was the first vice-president of design at Ford of Europe I worked under following my hiring by the company at Dunton in Essex in 1968. He'd arrived from head office in Detroit. Although of Romanian origin, Joe was 100 per cent American, right down to the way he dressed. This meant trousers that ended some eight centimetres above his shoes, which themselves featured very thick soles – all the rage in the USA at the time.

Joe had been responsible for the design of the first Mustang but had been effectively exiled to Europe by his boss, Eugene Bordinat Jr, who feared being overshadowed as the Mustang became ever more successful. But in actual fact the real reason was that both men had been in the running to replace the head of Ford Design, George W Walker, when he retired, and take up the role of vice-president of global design. And the last thing Bordinat wanted was to be working on a day-to-day basis alongside one of his former rivals.

Ford of Europe's design work was spread across two sites. Dunton in the UK handled interior design, alongside design work on all trucks, commercial vehicles and vans; there was also a small exterior design operation bound up with the creation of Ford of Europe in 1967, when Ford's British and German branches had different ranges of models. The other major centre, at Cologne in Germany, had lead responsibility for exterior design.

At the 1969 Turin motor show, Joe stood transfixed in front of the Ferrari 512S prototype. This was really something, he declared, and without a moment's hesitation he made a truly staggering offer to the prototype's architect, the designer Filippo Sapino. Sapino left Pininfarina right away and set himself up in a new Ford studio in Bruino, on the outskirts of Turin. But even though the Turin studio continued year after year to submit a good number of design proposals to compete for the various new programmes under way in Europe, none of these turned out to be very different from those presented by the Cologne or UK design centres. And for good reason: in reality there was only a single designer behind all of these projects: Joe Oros. As someone involved in the Brenda project for the successor to the first rear-wheel drive Escort of 1981, I could see that the fifteen or so design proposals were all the outcome of a near-incestuous relationship with their parent. Joe was a master of the art of grafting the front of one proposal onto the rear of another one, and by splicing in the bodyside design from a third study he was able to come up with a fresh proposal.

In 1973, a year before Joe returned to the United States, Ford bought the *carrozzeria* (coachbuilder) Ghia, until then owned by the Argentinian entrepreneur Alejandro de Tomaso. It was decided that Sapino would head up all the activities of the Bruino studio as well as those of Ghia; his team consisted of three designers, Delio Meinardi, Marinela Corvasce and the great Tom Tjaarda. I knew Tom well: among his designs was the De Tomaso Pantera, and he had worked on project Wolf, which became the Ford Fiesta. Unfortunately for Sapino, however, Tom's great talent was spotted by Fiat and, two years later, he left Ghia. I sensed this was something of a turning point, and from this time on the American influence began to gain too much of the upper hand, gradually diluting the Italian character of the *carrozzeria*.

Ghia had had a long history of working with American designers, including Virgil Exner, who went on to become head of design for the whole of Chrysler, and Tom Tjaarda, himself also an American. But in reality the problem lay in the purpose and timing of the American designers' missions to Italy: the visiting designers rarely stayed in Italy long enough to saturate themselves in the Turin ambience and become fully tuned in to Italian culture. The result was that their designs continued to show the imprint of Detroit's thinking. But, more than any other factor, it was the general directions provided by those in charge of Advanced Design that damaged Ghia: Advanced Design bosses had overall responsibility for all design activities outside the US, yet their frequent flying visits had the effect of undermining the Ghia studio and robbing it of its standing as a gold standard of Italian design.

While I was director of design at Ford in Germany in the early 1980s, Ghia would present one or two proposals for each new programme. I remember the moments when we unloaded the trucks and unpacked the models: we were taken aback by how ugly they were. Massively complicated in their styling, they had the disastrous proportions that very often go with unconvincing themes. Of course there were some notable exceptions, such as the fabulous Barchetta, presented in 1983. But even that, tragically, was later boiled dry into an awful residue that was eventually manufactured in Australia as the Capri SA30 cabriolet – a model that the world has thankfully long since forgotten.

I personally was witness to this descent into mediocrity and worse, which took place at the same time as a frenzied push on productivity: in 1974 alone, Ghia produced seventeen prototypes, and this figure was the most important element in satisfying the key performance indicators brandished by our American managers. This is how, bit by bit, Ghia began to become a kind of tuning shop, in much the same way as with George Barris, California's customizing king.

Henry Ford I might once have famously declared that 'history is bunk', but history itself very often proves that the opposite is the case. And just as history deserves to be respected, so it is vital to protect culture, too, and to go beyond purely superficial analyses. Because, even though ketchup and pomodori share the same colour, you'll find that when it comes to taste, they are rather different.

The Italian connection

Although most people associate Carrozzeria Ghia nowadays only with top-of-the-range Fords, it has been much more than that for more than a century. Indeed, it is (was?) one of the oldest *carrozzerie*, having been founded during World War I by Giacinto Ghia. In the years to World War II, Ghia established its name by producing, like Pininfarina, Bertone and many others, elegant designs that attracted upper-crust customers, especially when those designs were the work of young Mario Revelli di Beaumont. However, Ghia holds a special place in the history of automotive design for reasons other than the beauty of its products. To start with, Ghia always was an incubator for designers who, afterwards, pursued brilliant careers: after di Beaumont, Felice Mario Boano, Giovanni Michelotti, Pietro Frua, Giovanni Savonuzzi, Giorgetto Giugiaro and Tom Tjaarda all worked for Ghia at one time or another, creating hundreds of concept cars such as the 1967 Oldsmobile Thor, and production cars such as the dainty Renault Floride (Caravelle in the UK and USA) or the long-lasting Volkswagen Karmann Ghia. Then, Ghia was the first Italian coachbuilder to establish a long-lasting consulting relationship with American automakers, at first with Chrysler, then with Ford, which eventually became the owner of Ghia in 1973. Ironically, high-end Fords are now badged Vignale, a *carrozzeria* that was absorbed by Ghia in 1969.

In the Glass House

It is not often a topic of everyday conversation, but one of the key aspects in which car design has evolved over the past forty years is the changes in the size of the vehicle's glazed surfaces. Take the 1970s, for example: cars from that era had side windows that were positively gigantic in comparison with those on today's models. Note, too, that the cars' beltlines were parallel to the ground and to the sills, and that they sometimes dipped down into the doors to gain a few centimetres more window height. Some designers even went as far as to add a strip of bright trim on the doors in order to trick the eye into thinking the window areas were greater still. I have to confess that I did precisely that on the Ford Corcel, a car we designed for the Brazilian market after Ford bought out Renault's operations there. That car went on to prove a great success despite its Renault 12 underpinnings, which were far from the ideal base on which to build a beautiful car.

This was an era when designers spent a lot of time with their engineering colleagues seeking out the most ingenious ways of sinking the side window line as deep as possible into the doors. The idealized car, as displayed in concept sketches pinned up in every design studio worldwide, followed the same theme: a slender lower body, dominated by a tall glasshouse the height of which was totally disproportionate. The whole assembly was topped by a wafer-thin roof structure to give a panoramic 360-degree view, just as in a fighter plane. This quest for uninterrupted all-round vision was the logical conclusion of an old dream that began in the USA and which can be traced back to that great father of General Motors design, Harley Earl (see page 53), and his fascination with jet fighters – most notably the North American F86 Sabre. That aircraft provided the inspiration for a whole series of dream cars showing a strong aeronautical influence; these designs included the remarkable 1953 GM Firebird 1, which not only sported winglets and ailerons but also featured a cockpit enclosed by a proper glass bubble canopy.

There is one design that pushes the bubble theme to an almost caricature-like extreme: the American Motors Pacer. Launched in 1975, twenty years after Harley Earl's fantasies, its entire body was rounded – and the press soon dubbed it a 'goldfish bowl on wheels'. In sharp contrast to the Pacer's surface treatment came the unfortunate Renault 11 and its Renault 9 cousin, launched in Europe in 1981. Here, the style was boxy and angular, as if chopped from a block: both had glazed areas that were huge in relation to the designs' overall size, giving them a fragile and unstable look. This, by the way, did not prevent some six million examples from being sold. Well before that, there was the very pretty Simca 1300 of 1963, designed under the aegis of Mario Revelli di Beaumont: this, too, had generous areas of glazing, matched by a full, though tautly drawn, lower body, making for a very graceful overall look. Much the same theme was picked up by Hartmut Warkuss for the 1972 Audi 80 (which became European Car of the Year for 1973) and even by the first Volkswagen Golf, by Giorgetto Giugiaro, which came out two years later. All these designs are characterized by beltlines parallel to their sills, and by superstructures that to today's eyes seem disproportionately tall.

But it wasn't purely the desire to improve visibility that lay behind these constant endeavours to push beltlines downwards. Low beltlines also allowed the driver to roll down the windows, don sunglasses and place a nonchalant elbow on the bodywork and play the part of the all-conquering hero at the wheel of his or her steel steed. All these cars had one further thing in common: in summer they became hot – very hot – inside, for in Europe air conditioning was still the exclusive preserve of top-of-the-range models. On the other hand, children riding in the rear seats could see out and enjoy the countryside they were travelling through. But that, of course, was before the invention of video games, and today on a family outing the kids will often be hidden

The Ferrari 512S Berlinetta Speciale.

under a blanket, engrossed in their favourite video game and completely oblivious to what is going on outside. And usually, when the parents get all excited and try to attract their children's attention, perhaps on the approach to something splendid like the Millau Viaduct in southern France, the little philistines are likely to snap back: 'No, we can't be bothered, we've already seen it on TV.'

And this is how, to compress many years of history into a single evolutionary step, the influence of Harley Earl, which had been dominant for so long, came to be superseded by a new trend that had taken quite some time before being adopted by automakers: the wedge shape. First dreamed up at the end of the 1960s, the wedge finally displaced the dull, undynamic style of the era; most notable in triggering the shift was Bertone's Carabo design study. Yet, to this day, I still remain as captivated by the sublime Pininfarina prototype

designed by Filippo Sapino, the Ferrari 512S, as I was when I first saw it in 1969. This is one of the masterpieces of Italian design, characterized by a cuneiform or wedge-shaped profile and, starting at the nose, a character line that wraps round the front wheel arch to the three-quarter point. From there the line rises and accelerates in an exquisitely judged arc before finally flattening out at its high point over the rear wheels. As for the glazed areas, they are very narrow indeed, and the beltline – such as it is – follows the line of the wedge. It may be difficult to describe, but it is a thing of true beauty.

All this meant that, at a single stroke, the glazed areas had shrunk to almost nothing. It was almost as if a subliminal command had been issued: at the precise moment that the windows grow smaller, along comes air conditioning for the masses. How do you explain that one?

The invisibility cloak

It is often proclaimed that form follows (or should follow) function. But what does function follow? A need, or a wish? In this respect, the evolution of trends in designing glass areas in cars seems closely related to architecture. During the Middle Ages, both people's homes and fortified castles had small windows because a priority was protection, whether from the cold and rain, or from bombards and catapults. From the Renaissance onwards, while peace and prosperity increased, windows grew larger. In a way, this trend culminated with Joseph Paxton's Crystal Palace at London's Great Exhibition of 1851. Similarly, car windows and windscreens kept growing during the post-war period of prosperity: the driver of a 1960s Panhard 24 or of a 1970s VW Golf Mk1 enjoyed an incredible 360-degree visibility, and, in a way, Bertone's 1967 Lamborghini Marzal was an automotive Crystal Palace. Is it a coincidence, then, if glass areas started shrinking as oil crises, recessions, geopolitical changes and growing unemployment became the norm? Many of today's cars, like medieval castles, have loopholes rather than windows, as if driving offered protection from potential attacks. Even when the glass area remains correct, heavily tinted privacy glass is increasingly often used. Will tomorrow's autonomous cars have windows at all?

10

Fashion and the Automobile

Automotive style is like the waves on the shore, an incessant coming and going that leads nowhere but which nevertheless remains fascinating. And, as the French poet Paul Valéry wrote in the early twentieth century, 'Events are the spray on things. What interests me is the sea itself.' Which brings us to the mother of style, fashion. First, I would like to pass on what the great Italian designer and design theorist Bruno Munari said on the subject: 'Design is like making a pizza. You have to bring together all the correct ingredients and combine them in the right way. But style is the oregano, the final touch that's applied before the pizza goes into the oven.'

I am naturally not very comfortable with this definition, with its subtext that design needs a thin sprinkling of style to make itself attractive. For me, this stems from the outdated notion that remains in vogue in the media, which defines design as it was done in the 1960s, the era of the French designer Jacques Viénot, a celebrated figure in industrial aesthetics. He designed his industrial applications as if they had been conceived from a fine-art perspective, but in my view that's not design. In French the word *design* simultaneously encompasses both *dessin* (a drawing) and *dessein* (a design or project). It is associated with a process of creation centred on humans and how things are used. Yet human beings need a sense of coherence, of relevance, of harmony and of beauty, and this is what designers strive to imbue every project with, whether they are working on a lawnmower, a mobile phone or a car.

And where does fashion sit in all this? More strictly speaking, it should be fashions, in the plural, for fashions come and go, and then reappear, in a more or less regular pattern. Just like hemlines for skirts: the only certainty here is that they are subject to practical limitations. If you go beyond short, the skirt will no longer exist, and as for long.... Parallels in the world of cars might be shapes that are more rounded or more taut; voluptuous

volumes unmarked by creases, as in the Jaguar E-Type, or those with sharper feature lines, as in the DeLorean DMC-12.

Of course, there were times when the predominant profile for a car – at least for those not hand-built by a coachbuilder – was round, plump and occasionally bloated. This was particularly evident in the 1930s and in the post-war period: it was a consequence of the limitations of the manufacturing processes of the time. From the 1960s onwards, however, manufacturing technology took off rapidly. This is the glorious period when the Italian *carrozzerie* were at the high point of their influence: Pininfarina, Touring (see page 194), Bertone, Zagato and, slightly later, the brilliant Giorgetto Giugiaro, who would become a kind of emperor in the realm of automobile taste. Giugiaro was not quite like Nero, who in his day would stretch out on his chaise-longue in the arena stands and raise or lower his thumb; instead, similar judgements would be exercised with styling studies displayed at the Turin motor show. Concept cars such as Giugiaro's spectacular Maserati Boomerang in 1971 or his Ace of Spades in 1973 signalled the arrival of very structured forms. Likewise, everything changed in 1980 when, with his superb Lancia Medusa concept, the *maestro* decided it was time to move on to something different; this ushered in a new era of softness and fluidity.

At that time I was responsible for design at Ford in Germany and we had begun tooling up for the new Sierra model, which was very aerodynamic in its design and employed organic shapes very much ahead of their time. I must confess that at the opening of the Turin show we all breathed a deep sigh of relief when the covers were pulled off the Medusa. We felt reassured for the future, even more so as our big boss, Henry Ford II, had proclaimed his total rejection of our design. Mercifully, however, Mr Ford placed his trust in the freshly arrived head of Ford of Europe, the legendary Bob Lutz. And it should not be forgotten that in those days the development cycle for a new model took forty-two months

The DeLorean DMC-12 (top) and the Jaguar E-Type.

and that it was simpler to follow the herd than get ahead of it.

For many years we had been aware of the danger of a new stylistic orientation coming from a major coachbuilder, heralding a new trend and taking the industry in another direction: this could be devastating for an automaker who was at the point of launching tooling for a new model. Things have changed, thanks to the Japanese manufacturers: today, the development cycle has dropped from forty-two months to nineteen, something that helps to make the impact of decisions less black-and-white.

On the other hand, something that has become critically important to an automaker is to follow demand in the market and, better still, to anticipate trends – as Renault did in 1996 with the Scénic, the success of which brought in enough cash to buy Nissan. Equally, no one can now afford to turn a blind eye to the megatrends in the market, as was the case with SUVs, which French constructors took no notice of in the early 2000s.

Never forget, either, what Henry Ford I, founder of the brand that bears his name, is said to have declared: 'If I had asked my customers what they wanted, they would have replied: a faster horse.' Yes, it is wise to listen to your customers, but always keep your ear at a safe distance and, above all, never doubt your own instincts.

Fashion victims

What makes a colour, a shape, an accessory fashionable one day, and 'so last year, dear', the day after? The answer remains a mystery, whether it concerns clothes, food, or cars. With an important difference: clothes are put away in drawers and wardrobes, food is consumed, but cars remain in the street long after they have gone out of fashion, as an embarrassing reminder of what we craved for and now wish could be forgotten. Today vinyl roofs, plastic 'aerodynamic' add-ons and 1970s accessories look faintly ridiculous; the worst efforts of 1980s and 1990s 'bio-design' tend to offend our eyes; and it seems that we have finally understood that 'go-faster' stripes, matte-black bonnets and bright colours (or 'signal' as they were called in Germany) do not a faster car make. However, are we immune to fashion? This is far from certain. It is quite possible that in a decade or so, we – or our children – will smile about a time when cars were almost all painted in many shades of (metallic) grey, shod with absurdly large-diameter wheels and ridiculously low-profile tyres. And we might even wonder why we craved barn-like barges fit for crossing the Sahara, when our biggest motoring adventures were about driving 500 miles of motorway at a speed limit of 70 mph.

11
Cars for the Year 2000

I spent my entire youth in the year 2000. I grew up surrounded by businesses calling themselves '2000': Bar 2000, Mini-market 2000, 2000 Dry-cleaners and, just around the corner, 2000 Plumbers. This meant I was always living ahead of my time, even if it all finally caught up with me on 1 January 2000. All the better to propel me into the new millennium and look forward to 3000 Dry-cleaners...

The automobile, too, has always aspired to be ahead of its time. For those involved in creating cars it is an insult, bordering on defamation, to describe a newly launched model as being up to date or the flavour of the moment: during the product-creation process the designers are always fired up with optimism and the prospect of a great leap into the future. In the 1950s and 1960s, when the future still had a future, people thought that it would be atomic, that everyone would be issued with rose-tinted spectacles, and that happiness would be all around – that was the firm promise.

A good while before this, the French illustrator Albert Robida was one of the most brilliant predictors of the future. His *Sortie de l'opéra en l'an 2000* (*c.* 1902) shows us a futurescape of a sky above Paris, peppered with wonderful flying machines – limousines, taxis, buses, private aircraft – and you can even pick out a flying vehicle operated by a policeman dressed in the flamboyant uniform of a Republican Guard, directing the flow of aerial traffic. The illustration is packed with prediction: some of these flying machines are even being piloted by women, wearing trousers! On a more technical level, Robida's aerial craft are all large fish-like creatures, with pointed snouts and portholes for eyes, and they are all powered by the magical force of electricity, very much the excitement of the age.

My first encounter with a car for the year 2000 came courtesy of the astonishing Simca Fulgur. Named after the Latin for 'lightning', the Fulgur was designed by a young Robert

Opron for a competition organized in 1958 by the magazine *Le Journal de Tintin*; Simca was the only car company to take up the challenge. Drawing its inspiration from jet fighters, in particular the French-designed Fouga Magister with its butterfly tail, the Fulgur was supposedly powered by an atomic reactor; it had radar and was operated through voice control, everything being overseen by an electronic brain. The nuclear reactor aside, all these capabilities are very close to those of the autonomous cars that we are anticipating right now. Robert Opron went on to become the right-hand man of Flaminio Bertoni, father of the Citroën DS, and later took over as head of design at the *marque aux chevrons*. But his real claim to fame is as architect of that masterpiece of futuristic thinking, the Citroën SM – a design that has never been equalled.

When the Fulgur was unveiled at the 1959 Geneva motor show and two years later in Chicago, it followed a trend that was started several years earlier by General Motors and its Art and Colour department. Later renamed the Styling Section, it was directed by Harley Earl, a veritable giant in the pantheon of automobile design. In 1949 Earl had launched the first in a series of travelling Motorama roadshows, marshalling huge resources to present to the American public a vision of tomorrow's automobiles, cars that GM said pointed towards the year 2000. Motorama shows continued until 1961 and the dream cars they generated will always remain fascinating snapshots of that era.

Harley Earl and his petrol-head associates, drunk on high-octane leaded fuel, were obsessed with jet fighters, rockets and other symbols of power and speed. But, intriguing though their mobile creations undoubtedly were, they can be seen as total failures when it comes to predicting the designs of year-2000 cars; the latter, to the disappointment of many who had waited so long, proved to be sober and unexciting. Yet, on the other hand, today's cars do incorporate nearly all the technological gizmos imagined by our ingenious visionaries

The Simca Fulgur.

for the year 2000 - apart from the atomic reactors, of course.

The common element that unites all these creatives and their overflowing imaginations is that their ideas remain firmly rooted in the time in which they were conceived. Even if someone is ahead of their time when it comes to ideas, they can never escape the fact that those ideas will be constrained by present-day processes and the technologies associated with them. Style is by its very definition a thing of the moment; it follows that 'advanced style' is a contradiction in terms and can never exist. For proof, look no further than Leonardo da Vinci, the greatest designer who ever lived. He invented almost everything, often several centuries before others: from submarines to tanks and from aircraft to helicopters, his ideas and his concepts were way ahead of their time. But as for his designs, they have remained firmly anchored in the fifteenth and sixteenth centuries. Which goes to show that, when it comes to style, there's no escaping the mood of the moment.

Tomorrow never knows

Time fascinates and terrifies in equal measure, for we can measure and feel its passing, but we cannot control it. Our fear of time and of change is such that, as early as the second century AD, the Greek philosopher Sextus Empiricus even thought about denying the existence of time altogether: 'It is said that time is made of three parts, past, present and future. Among them, past and future do not exist: indeed, if times past and future did exist right now, they would be present.' So, what will tomorrow be like? Must we be terrified, or optimistic? Should we expect doom, or progress? People in the nineteenth and twentieth centuries believed in the latter to such an extent that disappointment was unavoidable. This disappointment translates in today's cars: the SUVs and 'crossovers' that swarm all over the world's roads promise to protect their occupants from the outside world, safely ensconced in a sheath of steel. In a way, they recall the Great Wall of China, the Maginot Line in 1930s France, Hadrian's Wall in England, and all those structures built in vain attempts to stop times from being, as Bob Dylan sang, 'a'changing'.

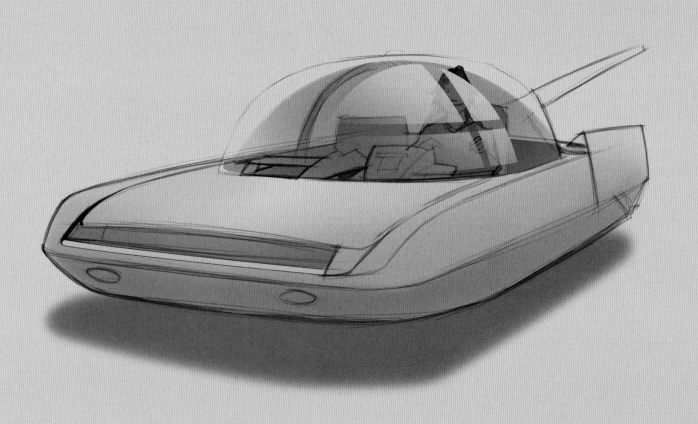

12
Moleskine and Insomniacs

LE GUÉMENT 1972

Henri Poincaré, the architect of chaos theory and one of France's greatest men of science, wrote in 1905 that 'a thought is but a flash of lightning in the middle of a long night, but this flash means everything.' Later, this came to be engraved on the medals issued by the CNRS, France's national science and research organization. It must be said that chaos is something that designers know all too well, and the same goes for night-time flashes. These ideas naturally seem brilliant in the midnight hour but by the next day they have generally disappeared into our virtual filing systems, ready to spring out again at any moment. Mercifully, in the midst of those many ideas there can be some real nuggets, still in their raw state but ripe for polishing up.

Ah, those thoughts that keep you awake at night and which, after you've dithered for ages, eventually force you to get up and go in search of a pencil and paper! Such middle-of-the-night thoughts aren't exclusive to architects and designers, to so-called creative professionals – far from it. Yet every designer I know has them, constantly; even if those thoughts are nothing to do with any particular issue or concern, many designers simply find it hard to switch off the engine, and it's all too easy to keep on coming up with improvements to the proposal that's being developed.

The automobile is still an object of passion, although this is becoming less true for some drivers. For some, traffic jams make it an effort to get from A to B: those drivers resent the feeling of getting nowhere and being stuck in an auto*immobile*. But in spite of all this, the automotive dream remains very real and, for evidence, look no further than museums. Each one of you has almost certainly been to an automobile museum or has heard of at least one such museum. But have you ever heard of a museum devoted to the refrigerator, the vacuum cleaner, or the hairdryer?

After many years of trying to resist getting up during the night to jot down a new idea, I ended up formalizing the ritual by placing on my bedside table a well-sharpened pencil, an eraser and a neat notebook held shut with an elastic loop. One consequence was that I would often spend more time out of my bed than in it and, with as many failed ideas as successful ones, the other outcome was ever-increasing bags under my eyes.

In the early 1970s the small progressive Ford design studio that I ran in Germany went by the name Forward Design, rather than Advanced Design. My boss, Uwe Bahnsen, had realized that in each of the numerous financial crises that this noble company had suffered, the cuts made by the cost accountants tended to land heavily on any activity that included 'Advanced' in its title. One day, Bahnsen asked me to stop all work on current projects without delay; instead, I was to respond to a request from a very influential German magazine, *auto motor und sport*. The publication had asked all the German domestic automakers to provide illustrations of how they would imagine the exterior and interior of a car for the year 2000. Not having any actual innovations to show, the magazine would use our illustrations within an extended article on the subject, set to appear at regular intervals. I decided to devote myself personally to this laudable task: I had always been passionate about anything smacking of futurism, I loved producing exciting renderings – and there were only two days to go before the deadline.

I spent most of the first day doing freehand sketches so as to pull in as broad a spectrum of ideas as possible; in practice this meant that I covered an entire display panel with drawings, ideas, schematics and drafts. And then I realized that I absolutely had to take a look at the work of that grand master of automotive science fiction, Syd Mead. His book had arrived from the United States a few days before, and leafing through its pages had the effect of a cold shower on me: Mead had done it all before, he had invented everything and, to make matters worse, his renderings were true works of art.

A rearranged composition of Patrick le Quément's 1972 drawing for *auto motor und sport*.

Disheartened by what I'd just found out, I headed back home and, uncharacteristically, dozed off for half an hour before returning to the task, attacking the work in a frenzy of creativity. That was how, in 1972, I came up with the concept of a vehicle travelling at 120 mph between Paris and Cologne, where I lived with my family. Among its many innovative features, the vehicle was equipped with a system which, well ahead of its time, used a network of transmitters embedded in motorway barriers for its guidance. Its largely digital dashboard featured an analogue display for speed, and in the centre was a larger read-out and a map, which not only indicated the vehicle's position in real time, but also showed the number of miles already covered as well as the remaining distance to the destination. With the benefit of hindsight it could be seen as spot-on in its functions but completely wrong on the technology. Visible on the drawing, which was later picked up by several publications, were small screens at either extremity of the dashboard: these provided rear vision for reversing. And lastly, there was provision for the monitoring of the vehicle's technical status, triggered remotely and capable of printing out a diagnostic report – in real time, naturally.

I finally managed to finish the gouache just a matter of minutes before it was due to catch the express post, and I confess that I found it impossible to sleep that night as my brain refused to let go. But the following night, after the creative euphoria had had time to subside, I slept extremely well.

Such stuff...

Although scientists have thoroughly researched and described the different stages of sleep, the experiences it provides remain mysterious to most of us. We humans spend roughly a third of our life sleeping, yet we never know for sure what the night will bring: dreams, nightmares, or flashes of consciousness. Worse, we often wake up with only a faint memory of what our brain produced unbeknown to us, and which we sometimes would love to recapture. Legend has it that, like many others before and after him, the German writer Johann Wolfgang von Goethe (who died in 1832) kept paper and pen by his bedside, in case inspiration should visit him while he was asleep. One night, he had a vision: the whole meaning of the world appeared to him. Feverishly, he wrote down what he had suddenly understood, then went back to sleep. In the morning, remembering what had happened, he reached for his notes to read what he had written. On the sheet of paper was... a single stroke. Whatever we try to capture of what night brings to us, the last word belongs to Shakespeare's Prospero in *The Tempest*: 'We are such stuff as dreams are made on, and our little life is rounded with a sleep.'

Moleskine and Insomniacs

13

Drop the Shadow

LANCIA

PEUGEOT

FIAT

AUSTIN

MORRIS

The 1950s were not a good time to be a stylist with a French car manufacturer. The industry was dominated by an engineering culture in which aesthetic designers in the body department struggled to make their voices heard. And even those so-called stylists could often be former technicians from the design office who, although known for being 'pretty handy with the pencils', carried little weight against the authority of the high-powered graduates of France's prestigious engineering colleges, especially the École Nationale Supérieure d'Arts et Métiers and the École Polytechnique. One such highbrow engineer, who was engineering director at Renault during the 1970s, went so far as to describe the role of the Styling section as 'dressing up the hunchback'.

This helps to explain the 'beauties' that were the Simca 1100 and Renault 6. Things were different at Peugeot; here, the Styling section employed a number of fine-arts graduates, although none had any training in industrial design. This meant that the designers were paid peanuts and their status was well below that of the qualified engineers. In effect, they were the men in the shadows.

That was an era when styling departments employed far fewer people than they do now. Henri Thomas, who was in charge of Peugeot's Styling section in the early 1950s, had a team of just four, only two of whom were stylists. That figure now seems minuscule in comparison with the many hundreds of people who work in today's design centres, but it is easily understood: French automakers faced major financial headaches in the aftermath of the war, difficulties that initially forced them into a policy of issuing only a single new model, though pre-war designs did continue. In fact, it was not until 1965 that Peugeot felt able to put a second model line into production: the 204. Previously, there had simply been no need for an army of people equipped with pencils and watercolours. Furthermore, the development cycle for new models was roughly twice as long as it is today; the stylists had even more

time as their work was essentially limited to upstream activities. The reality was that the follow-through of a model as it entered the manufacturing phase remained the exclusive preserve of the engineering department.

Jean-Pierre Peugeot first called on Pininfarina to develop the 403 in 1951. The 403 was a high-stakes programme that was so vital for the company that the Peugeot bosses could not afford the risk of an uninspired design from their design staff of two. Never forget, though, that Henri Thomas was a man of great talent: he was the father of the whole so-called 'fuseau Sochaux' series of streamlined Peugeots running from the 1935 402, the 302 of 1936 and 202 of 1938, to the 203 of 1948. Nevertheless, the risk remained.

The Turin-designed 403 proved to be such a big commercial success that by 1957 Peugeot had signed a design development contract with Pininfarina. However in 1960, just a few short years later, the euphoria vanished: as soon as the new 404 was unveiled it became clear to Peugeot that its design was line-for-line identical to a whole series of models for other automakers that had also used Pininfarina's services. The reason was simple. Peugeot had requested that its new saloon draw its principal inspiration from the fabulous Lancia Florida prototype that the designer had presented at the 1955 Turin motor show, and it turned out that Peugeot had not been the only car company to have been impressed by the Florida: several other manufacturers had gone to Pininfarina for their future designs and had also stipulated the same prototype as the inspiration. That's why a whole clutch of designs, all very close in style, appeared on the market at the same time: the Lancia Flaminia and Fiat 1800 and also the Morris Oxford and Austin Cambridge.

Peugeot was faced with a situation for which there was no immediate solution, but in order to protect itself from similar mistakes in the future it imposed new contract conditions which, from 1962, guaranteed design exclusivity across the entire European

The Lancia Florida (top) was the inspiration for a host of other marques' cars.

The actor Jean-Paul Belmondo, imagined as a hard-working French stylist of the mid-twentieth century.

market. Fortunately for all concerned, export business had not yet developed significantly on a European level: even so, this experience would weigh heavily on Peugeot's brand identity for many years, something that was clearly intolerable for the company. The whole sorry episode also became a cause for concern among the other French domestic manufacturers, who were still cooperating with Italian *carrozzerie*, whether Pininfarina, Touring (see page 194), Bertone, Zagato, Ghia (see page 41), Michelotti, or the young upstart Italdesign, established in 1968 by Giorgetto Giugiaro (see page 49). A further consequence of the affair was that French manufacturers, beginning with Peugeot but also Simca, Citroën and Renault, began building up their own in-house design divisions.

Although it took more than twenty-five years to become reality, what had to happen eventually did happen. Thus model programmes beginning in the early 1980s started to see design competitions between external design houses and the companies' internal design teams, and the internal teams began to be more successful. One unfortunate consequence was that the word would get round among senior management

and board members, and design decisions would as a result be taken under influence. In one example that I got wind of, when certain Renault directors came into the presentation suite to view all the design proposals submitted for a new programme, one was overheard quite shamelessly asking 'Which one is the Giugiaro proposal?'

In 1960 Henri Thomas was replaced by Paul Bouvot, who directed the evolution of Peugeot's design working hand in hand with Pininfarina in a skilfully managed partnership – even though I can imagine there must have been some tricky moments. But in the end it was Bouvot's successor, Gérard Welter, who had joined Peugeot design at the age of eighteen, who was to trigger the earthquake and bring in a new order. Welter's 205, launched in 1982 and with the GTI following two years later, was a masterpiece of automobile design and not only transformed the image of the Peugeot brand but, most importantly of all, also helped to save the company itself. This provided the signal for other designers to come out of the shadow of the Turin carrozzerie, too.

As for Renault, it would be a further ten-year wait until the Twingo – but that's another story (see page 76).

Defining designs

In a way, car styling is close to animal life: some species disappear after they have reached their ultimate point in evolution. No one ever tried to create another Citroën DS of 1955–75. Conversely, some others set a new standard after which a new breed will be born. The 1903 Mercedes Simplex was one of these milestones, as were the 1913 Vauxhall 30-98, the 1922 Lancia Lambda and the 1955 Lancia Florida bodied by Pininfarina. Originally intended as a showcase to demonstrate Pininfarina's talent, the Floridas (a coupé and three saloons were built) were so successful among the automotive community that they actually gave birth to almost two generations of cars. The 1957 Lancia Flaminia was obviously the first one, then Peugeot and BMC followed, and Felice Mario Boano was under the Floridas' influence when he designed the 1800/2300 Fiats. However, the Florida (which incidentally was also Battista Pininfarina's personal car) was still influencing car styling years later: witness the continuous crease along the sides and the rear window sweep of the 1963 Buick Riviera, of the 1960s Opel Kapitän, Admiral and Diplomat, and of the 1975 Jaguar XJS. These features became such a Pininfarina signature that the *carrozzeria* kept on using them to the end of the twentieth century.

Drop the Shadow

14
Secret Services Included

Back in 1983 the Dutch beer magnate Freddy Heineken and his driver, Ab Doderer, were kidnapped by a gang of five people in the Netherlands. They were released only after the payment of a ransom of more than £15m, negotiated by the family. Some while after this distressing episode I was contacted by the head of external relations for Ford Germany, where I was director of design. He explained that I was wanted for a top-secret mission: Freddy Heineken had ordered an armoured Ford Granada and had requested the design department's involvement in upgrading the interior. A meeting was arranged at Heineken's headquarters, and that is where I first met him. He was courteous and polite, but he knew exactly what he wanted. I realized pretty quickly that his motivation for choosing the Granada was to remain inconspicuous – no offence to my team and me, who had laboured long and hard to transform the old and very American-looking Granada step by step through a rejuvination programme inspired by the very beautiful 1971 Fiat 130 Coupé by Pininfarina. This was how the volume manufacturers tended to design their products at the time, drawing their influences from the most recent studies presented by the Italian *carrozzerie*.

Nevertheless, I never quite understood why Heineken decided to extend the wheelbase of the car when his aim was to go unnoticed. Each time I went to see him he was accompanied by his bodyguard, a former member of the secret service: the bodyguard's behaviour was just like that of Inspector Clouseau, so brilliantly played by Peter Sellers in *The Pink Panther* films, and this put me into a state of near paranoia. This 'Inspector Gadget' gave me a lot of advice on how to protect myself from criminals. One example was, never to stand in front of the doors of a lift so that if gunmen were to step out, I would be able to fire first. In my case, this was not much use as I was never armed – unless you count a well-sharpened pencil as a weapon.

But later on, as I gradually rose through the corporate ranks, I began to become more aware of the company's security services, and when I travelled to some of the world's security hotspots I reminded myself of the advice of 'Inspector Gadget'.

One incident took place in Johannesburg, South Africa. I was being escorted throughout my stay by a Latvian bodyguard, an ex-legionary who was as wide across the shoulders as he was diminutive in height. To my surprise he did not carry any weapon – except a scowl that acted as a warning not to try anything. But when we drove back to my hotel in the evening from the conference I had been hosting, we did not stop at a single red light. It was too dangerous to slow down, he said...

At another conference, this time in Mexico City, I was informed about the boundaries around the hotel where I could go for a stroll without having an armed guard alongside me. I had been warned never to ride in one of the Volkswagen Beetle taxis that swarm around the city like wasps, and in any case it struck me as a crazy idea to use a two-door car as a taxi: even with the front passenger seat folded, customers would have to perform contortions to get into the back. I later learned that this model was popular with criminals and extortionists. At the first red light an accomplice would jump in and, at knifepoint, force the terrified passengers crammed in the back to go round all the cash dispensers in the area to empty their bank accounts. The poor victims were allowed to keep just enough cash to get back to their hotel in another taxi. I imagine none would ever go near a Beetle taxi again.

But my most dramatic adventure with my 'men in sunglasses' close-protection squad took place in connection with the opening ceremony for Renault's São Paulo design centre in Brazil. I had been briefed beforehand on the importance of sticking to all the best-practice rules for personal protection: no conspicuous wristwatch, no wandering beyond the perimeter of the safe area, and all the rest. So as I got off the plane I was surprised to see

The Ford Granada.

that the transport I had been provided was an Espace IV, 'the only one in Brazil', as my bodyguard proudly told me. To me, this seemed to go against every rule of discretion. But that was not all: there were also two support cars, one to lead and the second to secure the rear; two armed men travelled in each car. The journey from the airport to where I was staying proved to be an epic one as the two escorting vehicles executed a beautifully choreographed ballet. When approaching T-junctions, the procedure was always the same: the vehicle at the rear would overtake the convoy in order to block the traffic at the junction; we would then turn into the new street, to be rejoined by the vehicle that had blocked the road and which then resumed its station at the rear of the convoy.

After high-risk missions such as these, each return to France required several days to readjust to the real world. And I often thought to myself what a pity it is that the basic rules of security precautions are not taught in the design schools. They could well prove useful.

Catch me if you can

The battle between sword and armour has been going on for ages. It also concerns the ways chosen by the leaders of the automotive industry to protect themselves. Their protection began to become an issue in the 1970s, when terrorism developed in Europe. This terrorist wave did not pretend, as it does now, to be religious; it was revolutionary, and aimed at destroying capitalism. Three groups made themselves famous: the German Rote Armee Fraktion (Red Army Faction), the Italian Brigate Rosse (Red Brigade), and the French Action Directe. When the AD murdered Renault's president Georges Besse in 1986, French industry leaders all felt threatened, and many resorted to being driven in armour-plated cars, sometimes with an armed escort. This author remembers being stuck in a traffic jam between the Peugeot 605 of the company's president, Jacques Calvet, and his bodyguards' 405 as a particularly unpleasant moment, especially when the bodyguards reached for their guns. In Italy, Fiat's Gianni Agnelli, who also was a choice target, used a rather different method to drive around Turin: whether in his beloved Fiat 130 estate, in his armour-plated Lancia Delta Integrale or in one of his numerous other cars, he drove himself as fast as he could, often ignoring traffic lights.

15
Speed is Dead, Long Live Allure!

In 1920 one of France's greatest twentieth-century historians, Marc Bloch, wrote: 'One distinct characteristic distinguishes today's civilization from the one it replaced: speed. This transformation has taken place over the course of a single generation.' The usual tendency is to assume that the automobile was responsible for this phenomenon. Wrong: it was of course the railways. Let's take the example of the journey between Paris and Toulouse, a distance of about 440 miles. In 1650 it would have taken thirty days in a horse-drawn cart to get there. A century later, the mail coach took eleven days, while by 1840 it was only three days, using a carriage and changing horses at each stage. Already ten times shorter, the journey time would shrink dramatically with the arrival of the train. By 1851 it had fallen to thirty-one hours, and by 1891 the voyage took just fifteen hours. One interesting observation: these early trains travelled at about 30 mph.

These days, speed is something that, above all else, scares people. In their day, our great-great-grandparents had a mixture of feelings about speed, ranging from fascination to sheer terror. Some of them even predicted that the body would crumble when faced with the huge pressures that speed would produce, resulting in premature death.

Yet well before the first petrol-powered automobile from Mercedes-Benz in 1885, most of the population had already formed a deep-rooted association between speed and the concept of progress. The same applied when it came to marching, too. In one of his works, the Austrian architect Adolf Loos, a brilliant observer of his turn-of-the-twentieth-century times as well as one of the pioneers of the Modernist movement in architecture, noted what he called the 'astonishing slowness' of the Austrian armies in the eighteenth century: they managed 70 steps per minute, while in 1904 the armies in his era marched at 120 steps per minute. Even on foot, speed is still a measure of progress. So the question then becomes this: what can one attribute

specifically to the automobile in the way that it contributed to the fascination with speed? Cars first appeared between 1890 and 1900 in the context of a broad spectrum of innovations, each hoping to transform society. In actual fact, what was truly innovative about the automobile was not its speed, for it took several years of research and development before cars were able to achieve the same performance as trains.

What really changed the game was that the automobile enabled individuals to choose where they wanted to go, changing their minds whenever they wanted to, and going from A to B according to their fancy. In short, the car allowed people to enjoy individual mobility – an altogether new concept. Thus it is important to stress that the speed resulting from the changes associated with the pre-automobile era is of an entirely different order to the speed experienced and felt thanks to the automobile itself. Thanks to the automobile, humanity would enjoy a new experience of speed, a sensation intimately bound up with personal freedom.

So, where do we now stand when it comes to this obsession with speed? Speed remains a very big presence in our modern lives, but its means of expression has changed. The automobile is no longer regarded as the ultimate symbol of speed – far from it. Road safety and traffic congestion have put an end to that era, to the regret of some. In terms of communication, the car hasn't been able to compete with the maximum speed offered by the internet, which is capable of compressing to almost nothing the time lapse between expressing a thought and its instantaneous reception somewhere else.

Yet with cars we have entered a period of irreversible slowing down. Very soon, we will be limited to driving at 20 mph in all built-up areas and 50 mph on country roads, just as we are limited on motorways. Could it be that common sense and social pressures will prompt us to travel in 'relax' mode until a big technological push opens up a new era, that of the autonomous vehicle?

What does all this mean for design? What will tomorrow's autonomous vehicles be like when it comes to their design? Smooth and anonymous blobs, perhaps, with all the personality of an aspirin tablet? Or, on the other hand, might we spark a new wave of creative innovation that will go back to absolute basics and rethink the whole universe of mobility? For decades everyone, myself included, has been designing cars that proclaim their speed through their expressive body language, even though that symbolism often amounts to misrepresentation. We have been turning a blind eye to everyday reality, with our dashboard instruments graduated right up to 180 mph - something that reduces the area of the speedometer available for reading the speeds we are actually doing.

Right now, it is high time to return to the drawing board, because speed is dead. So, long live allure!

Fascination and awe

Strictly speaking, speed is the ratio between distance and time. As such, it is probably one of the most defining concepts of the human condition, as opposed to the animal condition. Be it the snail (.03 mph top speed) or the peregrine falcon (240 mph when nosediving), animals are limited by their build and by their environment. Human beings, on the other hand, have always tried to overcome their natural limits, first by using animal (horse) power, then steam, electricity, petrol... This quest for speed led to travels, to discoveries, to conquests. It also induced fascination and awe in equal measure. In a poem published in 1856, Victor Hugo writes that 'Stars flew in the branches, Like a swarm of firebirds'. However, in the same period, Irish physician Dionysius Lardner stated that 'Rail travel at high speed is not possible because passengers, unable to breathe, would die of asphyxia.' Road speed, probably more than anything else, catalyzes this blend of addiction and fear. With the paradoxical conclusion that, while cars have never been capable of going faster than they can now, speed limits are enforced almost everywhere.

Speed is Dead, Long Live Allure!

16

All Cars Look the Same

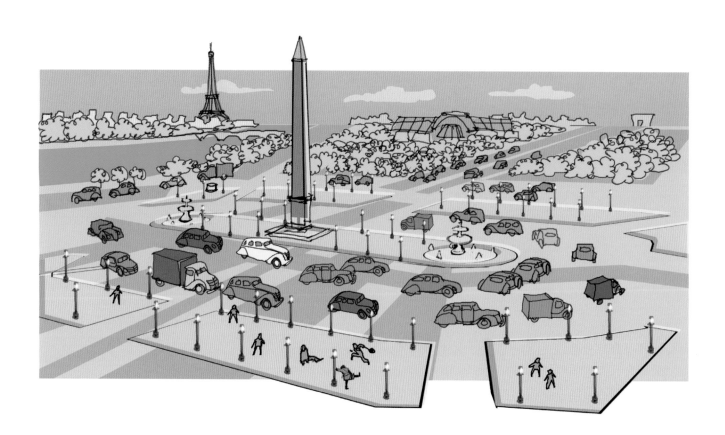

'Nowadays all cars look the same – it's not like it used to be.' I've been hearing this lament for several decades, even though it turns out not to be founded in reality but in a nostalgia for the so-called good old days. Because of course things were better then – or were they? How does truth sit vis-à-vis nostalgia?

A few years back I conducted an experiment, examining a series of archive photos of Paris's large and busy Place de la Concorde, taken at ten-year intervals between 1920 and 1980. After having dismissed all the cars that were not manufactured in the decade under examination, I came to the conclusion that the phenomena of imitation and follow-my-leader are nothing new. People who in good faith believe that cars from earlier eras showed greater differentiation than they do now are basing their opinion on Place de la Concorde playing host to vehicles spanning three or four decades.

Naturally, there are megatrends that flood through every era, sweeping away any semblance of non-conformism before finally enveloping everything in a reassuring blanket of uniformity. It's as true for cars as it is for fashion, for architecture, for furniture design. The mood of the moment is all-pervasive and permeates the thinking of designers too. So, what about examples from the world of automobiles? How many volume production models from the 1920s to the 1950s can you identify unprompted, or at least name the manufacturer? Maybe this is going back too far, so how about the 1960s and a comparison between the Peugeot 404 and the Austin Cambridge? Or repeat the exercise with the family sedans from European producers in the 1970s. And as for the decades from the 1980s to the present day, there is plenty of variety, freedom of choice still exists and nothing is yet prescribed.

Of course there are, and probably always will be, a number of creations that stand out from the crowd, the voices of which shout out loud enough to be heard above the background noise rather than miming along with the collective chorus. Cars such as those of Gabriel Voisin, the architectural C4, C11 and C14, set against a pre-war background of upright and uptight shapes; or Flaminio Bertoni's futuristic 1950s Citroën DS standing in sharp contrast to the American-inspired styling of the Simca Vedette Versailles, the highly conservative bulbous Renault Frégate or the pleasant if somewhat over-bodied Opel Rekord. And – why not? – the Avantime from Renault, another model with no direct counterpart (see page 120). Nonetheless it is important to recognize, even if the truth makes for uncomfortable reading, that none of these vehicles had any influence whatsoever on the rest of the automobile world. The DS is the perfect example of this: after the DS came nothing. There was never any post-DS follow-up, either from Citroën (the CX had nothing in common with its predecessor) or from other companies.

And then there is the reality that all the automakers tend to copy one another – after having first criticized the competition and discredited its product. Pacing the aisles of a motor show, you will never get the CEO of brand X, nor even the chief designer, to admit that the latest product from brand Y is in any way interesting. Yet as soon as they are back at headquarters they will begin shamelessly copying that product. Take BMW, for instance: the list is long of those who lambasted the company during the era of Christopher Bangle's designs (such as his Z9 Gran Turismo concept presented in 1999, which inaugurated an unusual sculptural treament known as 'flame surfacing', or his 2001 X-Coupé concept that hinted at SUV-like proportions), yet who went on to ape those designs. This shows that car design can often require three eyes: the first an eagle eye overseeing the neighbour's back yard, the second fixed on the past in the rear-view mirror and the third focused on market testing.

The market testing in question takes the shape of mysterious secret ceremonies that place the company's styling proposals alongside competitor models in the same location, the idea being to single out the least polarizing of the new proposals as the winner. A few years ago, this methodology involved stripping the badging off the competitors so that brand image wouldn't play any part in the decision. This left the competitors' cars up against the two or three rival design studies for the final choice. To no one's real surprise, it emerged that 30 per cent of those called on to pass judgement could no longer recognize their own car. No logo, no recognition: what a way to dent the pride of those brand image specialists! Yet as they are often the same people as those who present the results of the tests, honour is preserved – and originality is put on the back burner at the accessory shop.

A word of warning about these marketing tests, also known as clinics, came from David Ogilvy, head of the prominent advertising agency Ogilvy & Mather until 1973. 'The majority of companies', he declared, 'use clinics like a drunkard uses a lamppost – more for support than for illumination.' Thank you, David: I often had cause to quote you.

Copycats

Oscar Wilde once wrote that 'Imitation is the sincerest form of flattery that mediocrity can pay to greatness.' Indeed, when considering automotive design, originality does not seem to rule. Which is quite understandable, actually: if it ain't broke, don't fix it. The 1937 Opel Kadett and Renault Juvaquatre, for example, were next of kin. Similarly, the flowing and curvaceous lines of the 1936-37 BMW 327 and 328 had a significant impact on two British car manufacturers: Bristol blatantly copied the former with its 1947 400 (which, incidentally, also used the BMW's engine), and Jaguar's William Lyons took inspiration from the latter to design his 1948 XK120. Sometimes things can go even further: it is hard to believe that, in the 1950s, Pininfarina was not inspired by the austere Alfa Romeo 1900 Berlina when designing the equally dull Peugeot 403. The line between inspiration and imitation can be a fine one. It is less so in other cases, as demonstrated by the designs of the 1950s Packard Caribbean vs the Soviet Tchaïka, and of the 1990s Citroën Xantia and Daewoo Espero, or more recently by the Chinese Shuanghuan Bubble compared to the Smart Fortwo. Indeed, the Chinese automotive industry is full of unabashed copies, but it is not the only one.

All Cars Look the Same

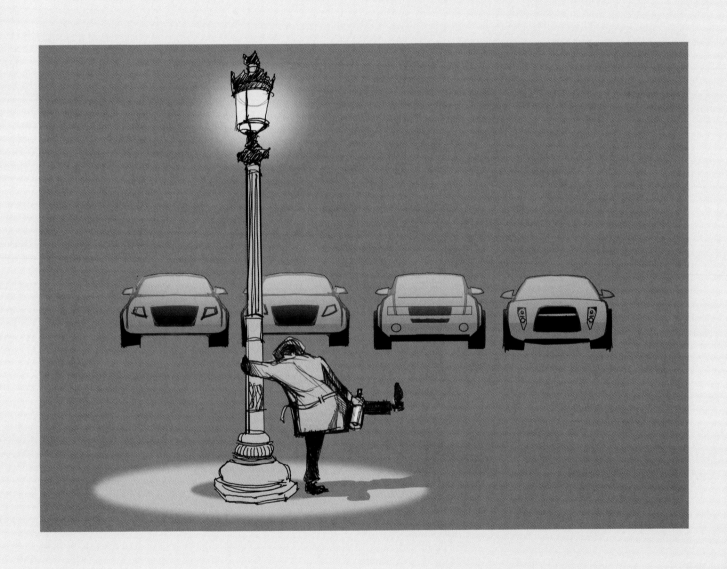

17
Instinctive Design and Extinctive Marketing

The first time I met Raymond Lévy, the head of Renault from 1986 to 1992, we straightaway established a strong connection. It was at his home in 1987, and we were meeting to discuss my joining the company. I lived in Germany at the time, and was preparing to become the very first director of design for the Volkswagen-Audi group. I was immediately struck by Mr Lévy's animated manner and his sense of humour, but most of all it was the clarity of his foresight that impressed me: his vision of what he felt my role could be in this great company. Mr Lévy had recently been called in to fill the shoes of his friend and predecessor at Renault, Georges Besse, who had been assassinated by the terrorist group Action Directe.

As I was talking to him about design, Lévy insisted that he did not know anything about it. Nevertheless, he recalled being sold a toilet brush at the Foire de Paris innovation show on the basis that it was 'very designer-label'. There was then a short silence, after which his face broke out into a knowing smile.

The conversation that followed centred principally on Renault and its heritage as a highly innovative marque when it came to vehicle concepts, some of them genuine game-changers. As evidence I cited its automotive milestones: for example the 1960s 4L, the first volume production multipurpose vehicle able to switch roles between a rugged family car and a small van, as well as being equipped with a hatchback tailgate; and the R16, with the remarkable flexibility of its interior and its versatility. I also pointed to the brilliant 1980s R25, with its innovative technology, and the charming little R5 which, with its plastic bumpers front and rear, instantly made every other production car seem out of date. And, lastly, the Espace of 1984, a project developed jointly with Matra and which triggered the emergence of a whole new market sector: one-box MPVs – people-carriers or minivans.

Renault had always fascinated me because it was an innovative company, and on numerous occasions I had considered applying to work there, before abandoning the idea for various reasons. But this time, I was called to meet its CEO because the head of design, the highly respected Gaston Juchet, wanted to retire. And that was how I came to be at the home of President (as company heads are titled in France) Lévy in a suburb to the west of Paris, not far from where I live today.

Lévy's vision was for Renault to regain its standing as an innovator, as the company had been before and immediately post-World War II. It was not for nothing that the company's founder, Louis Renault, became known as 'Mr A Thousand Patents'. I left the meeting having accepted Lévy's offer. He had gone much further than simply agreeing to my sole condition, that the styling division should report directly to the company's top management, rather than being a subset of the engineering operation; in addition, he promised me carte blanche to create an industrial design division, the mission of which was to help reposition Renault as a manufacturer of groundbreaking vehicles.

In December 1987, just before Gaston Juchet retired as head of the styling division, he handed me the keys to two lock-up garages. Stored in these lock-ups were two design proposals from a small-car programme that Georges Besse had cancelled on the grounds of poor profitability. I had these models brought in and was immediately bowled over by the potential of one of them. This proposal, though a long way from being finished, was the work of a brilliant young designer by the name of Jean-Pierre Ploué, under the direction of the late Jean-Francois Venet. It was somewhat undersize and had a rather ugly nose, but its one-box silhouette gave it unrivalled interior space and a remarkable sense of freshness.

With the support of product director Jacques Cheinisse we were able to convince Lévy to put together a team of technicians from the engineering division to establish the project's technical feasibility and begin to turn this little flea-like object into a car that would be intelligent – and profitable.

Doodles of the Renault Twingo.

The business case presented at the first big project meeting was far from convincing, despite the very best efforts of the talented programme director, Yves Dubreil. But then, after I had shown the model to Lévy and his team, and explained that this car should be thought of as a family pet that people would want to pick up and take indoors to bask in the warmth of the fireplace, Lévy quickly understood the metaphor and smiled – to which the model responded with its own smile. Some people said that this smile indicated that the adventure should continue, even though everything else suggested that the model should be locked back into its storage box.

Further down the line in its development, we put our car, the Twingo, into test marketing clinics at which several hundred people were asked to rate it in comparison with vehicles from competitors. The results were crystal clear: 25 per cent adored the car, and a further 25 per cent said 'yes, maybe', the subtext being that they did not want to be the first in their street to drive this car. The final 50 per cent were openly hostile. When these results were presented, I found myself confronted by a group of senior executives firm in their insistence that the Twingo's caricature-like style must be altered and the self-satisfied smile wiped off its face. I countered that argument, saying that the 25 per cent of people inspired with enthusiasm seemed to me to be a good foundation for success, whereas the only thing my opponents had latched onto was the 50 per cent negative response.

I left for the South of France for a long weekend to get some perspective on the matter, and on my return I sent Lévy a short handwritten note in which I asked him to choose 'instinctive design rather than extinctive marketing'. He returned it having appended 'Agree with you 100 per cent, Monsieur le directeur.' And that is how Raymond Lévy came to steer Renault onto its path of innovation. The Twingo was launched in 1992.

The fine line

In the beginning of the twentieth century, marketing automobiles was pointless: when a new product truly satisfies a widely shared need, most of the time its success is guaranteed and the main problem is to produce enough of it. However, things get trickier as soon as supply becomes greater than demand and competition arises between brands. Trying to understand customers' needs is not simple; trying to figure out the desires that trigger purchase is even more complex. The large investments for the launch of a new product can also be daunting, which explains why marketers often tend to favour only slight changes to products and to shun breakthroughs that could turn into failures. Still, being too cautious can also be dangerous, and research that is too heavy can be disastrous: there was absolutely no rational reason for the late 1950s Ford Edsel to become a historic flop. Conversely, no sane marketer would ever have advocated launching such unusual cars as the VW Beetle, the Citroën 2CV or the Morris Mini. Whatever the efforts (and whatever amounts of 'big data' used), marketing will never be a science; like economics, it explains fairly well what has happened, but cannot foretell much.

18

The Team Has Replaced the Solitary Genius

'Sure... but who *actually* designed the car?' That question was regularly put to me on new-model launches in hushed whispers by journalists in search of a scoop – the subtext of course being that there was an injustice that the reporter was determined to put right. After all, it is a typically French attitude to spring to the defence of not only widows and orphans but also those unfortunate designers starved of the oxygen of media glory and forced to slave away on the lower decks of the rowing galley known as the Design Centre. The broader public still clings onto the stock image of the designer as an artist, a sensitive soul hard at work in an environment dominated by inflexible engineers, autocratic marketing bosses and a corporate structure that banishes the hapless creative back into his or her box as soon as the spotlight of media acclaim is plugged in.

One of my first tasks as a rookie designer was to come up with a piece of chrome trim to embellish a car that was devoid of charm: the Simca 1100. At the time, it was customary for designers to start their careers with insignificant assignments: a hubcap here, a door handle there, perhaps an alternative frontal treatment or a variation on the bodyside profile. And then one day, once locked irreversibly into this career path, they could earn their rite of passage into the big time with a first project that might just be transformed into a life-size design model.

Ever since joining the ranks of design centre directors I have worked hard to banish these old practices and to allow young designers to express their ideas right across the board as soon as they become part of the team. Working alongside experienced designers and studio managers, with their ideas then run past the critical eyes of the head of design, new recruits can feel the buzz of having designed their first car. So much the better, although in actual fact they could not have done it without the whole team framework, the amazing talents of the digital modellers, the clay modellers and all the technicians and engineers whose job it is to ensure a project fulfils its design specification.

Over the course of the years as these designers are nourished and energized by the creative environment, they can become regular and productive contributors to the process, even if not everyone can become a powerhouse of innovative ideas. A notable example from my own experience was a Japanese designer who was one of the brightest stars of the design centre in Germany that I ran at the time. After switching companies, he suddenly found himself much less appreciated. The simple truth was that he no longer had the benefit of an environment that fed his creativity.

But to return to our original question: who else, apart from designers, has the greatest influence on the design of any new project? At the end of the day, the headline responsibility lies first and foremost with the person in charge, the CEO of the company: this is the person who deserves the praise. The role tends to go unrecognized by the general public and is seriously underestimated by the media in general. The CEO is present when all the most important choices are made, and it is of course the CEO who makes the final decision, too. Let's dig a bit deeper: who else has contributed to the design, and whose names should appear in the credits? Well, everything depends on the public: if the newly launched vehicle is a tremendous success, the press will ferret out a surprising number of names of people whose influence was judged crucial. After all, it is often said that success has a great many fathers, but failure is an orphan. So, if the new vehicle turns out to be a commercial flop, its architect will be whoever has to take the blame. And that, let's face it, is often the overall head of the design operation.

It can even happen, albeit rarely, that a designer can engineer his or her reputation on the basis of the wrongful attribution of the authorship of a project. I can remember the case of one young designer whose exterior style proposal for a concept car was

Enzo Ferrari.

Jean-François
Venet (centre) and
his team at work
on Renault's Scénic
concept car.

accepted. That in itself could be counted a significant success, given the designer's lack of experience. But, spurred on by a thirst for status, this person burnished their story along the way; artful story-telling inflated the tale, from being given responsibility for both exterior and interior design, to being head of an imaginary project and, finally, the designer and sole creative force behind a concept car. And this, in turn, was going to inspire a production model that would prove to be a huge success and a real cash cow for the manufacturer. Later, I went on to discover that according to this designer's CV published in a foreign magazine, they had been recruited as a departmental director, even though they had only just finished college at the time. As the nineteenth-century French humourist and writer Alphonse Allais said, 'once you've overstepped the mark, there are no longer any limits.'

By the same token, it must also be acknowledged that certain managers sometimes claim the full credit for projects in which they participated as young designers, barely out of college, failing to acknowledge they had enjoyed the advantage of huge support from the team. However, it can also be the case that, much later on in their careers, others try to claim the entire creative credit for projects in which they led a team. Even if their influence was the determining factor, I maintain that in today's industry design has become a collective activity carried out in the context of a collaborative community that works by bouncing creative ideas back and forth.

And I return once again to one of my heroes from yesteryear, but also so modern, the late racing driver and entrepreneur Enzo Ferrari, who declared: 'The team has replaced the solitary genius.'

Whodunnit?

In the same way that we need scapegoats, we need heroes, even if choosing people who deserve the title is always a bit unfair: in 1940, Winston Churchill was not the only one to stand against Nazism; neither was Bobby Charlton the only player of the English team to win the 1966 World Cup. The same goes with masterpieces, whether in art, technology or design. History did not retain the names of the amazing stone carvers who decorated France's Amiens cathedral; many of the great Flemish painters of the Renaissance were granted by the Guild of Saint Luke the permission to hire apprentices who would complete their paintings; and Enzo Ferrari built his fame on cars he did not conceive. Does this mean that there are no authors, no artists? Of course not. However, contrary to what happens in music, there are probably more conductors than musicians in automotive design. To say that the success or failure of a car is a single person's responsibility is as meaningless as pretending that Wilhelm Furtwängler deserved sole credit for the rendition of a Beethoven symphony by the Berlin Philharmonic orchestra.

19

The Keys to Design

In the early twentieth century, when asked what were the three most important criteria when buying real estate, Lord Samuel, the king of British property, famously replied 'location, location, location'. Today, if someone asked about the three key criteria for designing a beautiful car, I would answer 'proportions, proportions, proportions'. From the 1950s through to the 1970s there were several Italian GTs, somewhat ornate in their style, that would never have attracted any attention had they not been blessed with splendid proportions, low and wide for their time. An example? The 1955 Alfa Romeo 1900 CSS, designed by Felice Mario Boano. If it had been built on the platform of a Peugeot 403, the design would have been plain ugly, but the proportions of the Alfa chassis were its salvation. Conversely, even the sublime lines of Pininfarina's Lancia Flaminia study could not overcome the awkward proportions of the antiquated architecture of the Austin Cambridge, inspired by the Flaminia but sitting too high and too narrow on its wheels.

In the world of the automobile, the recipe for classical beauty begins with a body that is both wide and low. That is why today's concept cars are so fond of outdoing one another when it comes to these two dimensions; on occasion, you could be forgiven for thinking that the width of the design had been measured with an elastic tape measure. Because everyone else does it too…. Another clever trick, already widely exploited in the 1930s, is the art of the photographic setup. The brilliant Robert Doisneau used this to remarkable effect in his overhead shot of the dumpy Renault Viva Sport in a Parc de Saint Cloud street. At the wheel was a pretty but diminutive woman, barely 1.4 metres tall. The illusion was perfect and did wonders for the status of the car: anyone would have believed it to be an enormous Hispano-Suiza.

The elastic tape measure phenomena also applies when a manufacturer needs to choose between several design proposals that are up against one another; some may come from the in-house design department, others from an Italian design consultant. The temptation to shave a few centimetres off the height of the model is a strong one.

'*Miracolo, miracolo.*' Those words would often be heard in connection with a certain Italian designer of some renown. This consistently great creative was also something of a clever fox. I remember one design selection when, after we had checked that all our internal proposals conformed to the dimensions in the specifications, our Turin friend arrived, just a bit too late, after the in-house package engineers had gone home. 'Problems at the border in Ventimiglia. Those French customs officers!' At the end of the day, his design was the one selected, thanks to its superior proportions. Quite a while later, once the design had been adjusted to the correct dimensions (and after the designer had cashed our cheque), we realized that a great deal of its charm had evaporated. It was as if you had washed your favourite polo shirt at the wrong temperature and its striking yellow had turned an insipid beige. So much for skilfully contrived proportions and Latin-style *eleganza*.

To create a beautiful vehicle you need excellent designers, digital modellers and clay modellers. You will also need a package engineer who is well steeped in automotive culture and who is a passionate 'car person'; they must be open-minded and prepared to have their ideas challenged. It is perfectly possible to make cars that are 'intelligent' in a practical sense, but creations that are both intelligent and beautiful are few and far between. In truth, you can't play tricks with proportions. It is certainly possible to make do with them and to minimize their influence by adding feature lines along the carefully sculpted surfaces. But you can never turn a carthorse into a racehorse – and that's not in any way a criticism of the characteristics of an elegant Percheron.

While I was working at Ford in the United States in the 1980s the product director was an accountant with aspirations of becoming

The Renault Viva Sport.

An interpretation of
Leonardo da Vinci's
'Vitruvian Man'
(known in Italian as
'The Proportions
of the Human
Body According to
Vitruvius') applied
to car design.

the super-brilliant product person that he plainly was not. His idea was to create a new model based on the platform of a vehicle in the segment below; this new model promised spectacular levels of profitability, just as long as we could convince our customers (who were pretty canny) that the car was not in fact horribly narrow and misshapen. With double helpings of chrome and bucketfuls of glitter masking the car's lack of natural grace, the company would once and for all be able to turn itself around and everyone would strike it rich…. The car proved to be a commercial disaster, undermining the company's credibility and putting the brakes on the meteoric rise of our sorcerer's apprentice, who was forced to return to his first love, cost control. If, as Le Corbusier stated, 'proportions are what make objects smile', this proves that the opposite also holds true: bad proportions can be fatal.

The illustrator, the dwarves and the doll

Size does matter. If miniaturization seems to be a permanent target for some technological products (as shown by the entire history of watchmaking and of electronics), such is not the case for cars. For a good reason: cars have always been – and actually remain – symbols of social status, just like houses. And, also like houses, the bigger cars are, the better, at least within reasonable limits. In Europe, where engines were small, roads were narrow and steel was expensive, until recently most cars were cramped and oddly proportioned. Hence the long-lasting fortune of such gifted European illustrators as Alexis Kow and Eric de Coulon, who worked in the first half of the twentieth century. In their hands, even the most modest car was transformed into a full six-seater. To get that result, they cheated both on the proportions of the car, which they drew much wider and lower than it actually was, and on that of the people, who were as unrealistically proportioned as a Barbie doll. Photography made this (sometimes not-so-) subtle art of transformation more complex, but it is certainly still essential.

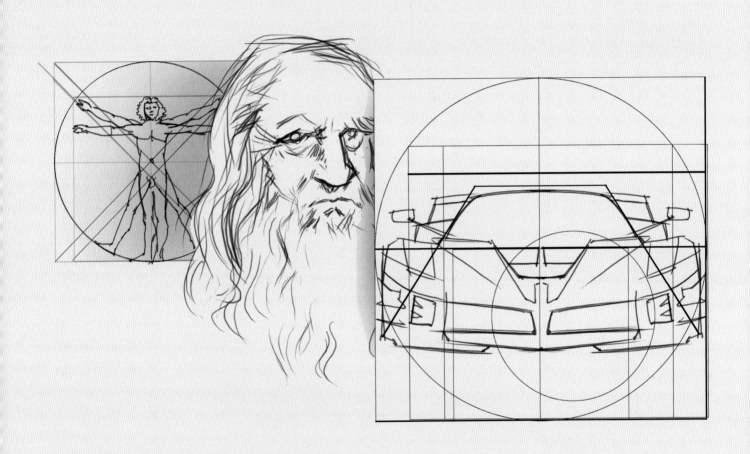

20
Belle Linee and Schöne Formen

When trying to describe a beautifully designed car, most French-speaking people will spontaneously say that it has *une belle ligne*, or a nice line. What matters is the graphic quality of the features, more than the shape itself. Focusing on lines underscores the importance of not only the silhouette, but also the lines that radiate from the intersections of volumes – lines that designers refer to as creases. In Italy, too, *belle linee* is the key expression used to describe a Ferrari. Surprisingly, though, a 250 GT SWB or a 250 GT Lusso are both strikingly beautiful because of their three-dimensional sculptural harmony, despite not being structured with character lines.

However, in the UK – where everything is of course different – people say that their cars have 'a beautiful shape'. Obviously, the organic, seamless E-Type Jaguar is what spontaneously springs to mind. More spontaneously, anyway, than, say, the 1960s Riley Elf or the later Austin Maxi. Like the French Citroën Ami 6 or Renault 12, these cars can be seen as rather embarrassing branches in our automotive family trees. As for the Germans, they also refer to beautiful shapes, or *schöne Formen*.

What lies behind those differing expressions? Many things, in fact. For decades in the mid-twentieth century, Pininfarina-penned lines were seen as the epitome of automotive elegance. Indeed, French and Italian *carrozzerie* put all their genius into the lines and into the two-dimensional graphic quality of their work. The Germans, on the other hand, were the *Meister* of full and balanced shapes. In consequence, popular wisdom in the 1950s had it (and somehow still has it) that Mercedes used thicker and stronger steel than Citroën or Fiat.

In the early 1970s I was working in a German design centre. There, I was in a perfect position to discover the amazing craftsmanship with which designers, modellers and draughtsmen laid out the fullsize line drawings from which all the industrial tooling was created. They knew how to balance and master the smallest radii to provide the impression the tooling had been milled out of solid billet, instead of having been simply stamped out. Each and every panel shouted 'Our cars are well-made, *Deutsche Qualität*'. This was the result of a typically German point of view: *konsequent zu sein*, be consistent, always, so as to provide the complete car with a reassuring feeling of robustness.

Is this a case of cause and effect? Until the mid-1980s, French and Italian designers made their styling models out of plaster, which does not lend itself easily to detailing since it is difficult to add material to it. Worse, plaster volumes are difficult to assess as they offer a matt surface, which can only be correctly appreciated in the early-morning daylight. Meanwhile, British and American designers were already using clay, a miraculous material. Matter can be easily added or removed from clay. Clay can be finely and precisely sculpted with the right instruments; it can be covered with a coloured plastic film called dinoc to provide a realistic surface. By the early 1990s clay had replaced plaster everywhere. Today, computer-controlled lathes and drilling machines provide complete control and have given birth to new aesthetics, with the car body considered as a unified whole.

Lines; shapes; what else? Colours, of course. But therein lies the rub: do we all see them the same way? Is your red my red? Is your red the same as the tomatoes my aunt grew in her garden? Nothing is an absolute certainty.

When I started studying design, I was lucky enough to have Naum Slutzky as my mentor. He was an old man by then, but in the 1920s he had been a teacher in the most important design school of the twentieth century, the German Bauhaus. Slutzky taught us to see things in a different way, and to stop opposing features and shapes. I remember that, during a drawing lesson,

The Alfa Romeo 6C.

Naum Slutzky and
the Bauhaus building
in Dessau, Germany,
where the art school
was based from 1925
after its move from
Weimar. The building
was designed by
Walter Gropius.

as we were working on a still life, he suddenly called for a break and asked us to do a surprising task: he wanted us to draw the space between the objects, instead of the objects themselves. This exercise changed our view of the world forever.

Nowadays, when I contemplate an elegant Touring-bodied Alfa Romeo 6C, I can see that its lines are incredibly fluid, that its volumes are both full and emotional, and that the shapes that form themselves between the car's silhouette and its environment are simply breathtaking. It's all in the looking...

Bauhaus

Bauhaus! For a non-German speaker, the word sounds like an explosion. For those who speak German, it is much more meaningful, though no less sonorous: Bauhaus means building (*Bau*) house (*Haus*). Indeed, building was of the essence in Germany in 1919, when architect Walter Gropius became head of the arts and crafts school that Henry van de Velde had founded in Weimar eighteen years earlier. Germany was in ruins after World War I, and the clamour of the Russian revolution had replaced the sounds of the artillery. In this world of violence, Gropius and the other Bauhaus masters shared an ambition: to give an aesthetic value to industrial products, from the smallest domestic appliance to the tallest skyscrapers and, of course, to cars. Indeed, Gropius designed a few cars for Adler. Although intense, the history of the Bauhaus was short. The school was too cosmopolitan, too open to the world, too conscious of social issues for the Nazis, who closed it in 1933. However, its masters, including Naum Slutzky, emigrated and spread their principles throughout the world. The Bauhaus staff list reads like a hall of fame for early twentieth-century design and art: László Moholy-Nagy, Paul Klee, Wassily Kandinsky, Marcel Breuer, Ludwig Mies van der Rohe...

21

High Tech Vs High Touch

What is good design? This is the all-important question discussed in the book *Design: Intelligence Made Visible* (2007), written by Stephen Bayley, cultural critic and the first director of the Design Museum in London, and Terence Conran, the celebrated designer-entrepreneur and founder of Habitat and of the Design Museum. They seek to answer the question through the lens of a maxim drawn from the architect Le Corbusier, 'Good design is intelligence made visible.' To which the authors add: 'Something that has not been intelligently designed will not work properly. It will be badly made, look depressing and be poor value for money... You would be stupid to want bad design.'

Good design really is intelligence made visible and, according to the formula, is made up of 95 per cent common sense and 5 per cent of a mysterious, even magical, quality that is best explained as the emotion triggered by the aesthetics. We're talking about the whole entity here. An iPhone is attractive in its entirety, thanks to its shape and the materials it is constructed of, as well as its intuitive operating solutions and the quality of its graphics – all of which have made it such a spectacular success. Good design really shows, and it makes you want to touch it.

I remember the design director for a large car brand who would say to his young designers: 'If you want to truly understand the shape of a car, try washing one. Incidentally, my own car happens to need a clean, so let's move on to a practical exercise.' While it is possible that he saw this ploy as no more than a means of getting a free car wash, there is still a lot that rings true in his suggestion. Blindfolded tactile exploration of the curves on a fender, following the fluid course of a character line, sensing the tension in the vanes of a grille – all while washing the boss's car: that's a great real-life lesson that can pay big dividends later. That's not an exaggeration: an Indian car-designer friend recently told me how he went to the Tokyo motor show and was surprised to find that of all the worldwide brands gathered under that huge roof, the only marques that he felt like actually touching and stroking were the Renaults, Peugeots, Citroëns and DSs.

Much the same applies to the design of vehicle interiors, too. But here it goes much deeper because we are now dealing with notions of how to embrace the various shapes of the human body; for example, the form of a gear-lever knob that must reflect the palm of the hand. In a similar spirit, we are also beginning to approach the related subject of the vehicle's technological welcome, with a particular focus on 'simplexity', something I have been advocating for a long time. A combination of simplicity and complexity, simplexity is a term I first used in 1999, with the aim of ensuring that simple things remained simple, while also making complicated things accessible. How many times have you been baffled by an instruction saying something like 'press the lower button three times, while hopping on your left foot and singing "God Save the Queen"'? (I exaggerate, but not by much.) Many instruction manuals appear to have been written by a secret society of techno-sadists.

Whether in the world of business or that of design, reference is often made to the concept of 'the French touch'. A uniquely French approach that combines intelligence, pragmatism and a sense of creative freshness and originality, the French touch leads to the employment of 'touch design', as opposed to the high-tech approach. Touch design could be applied in the interiors of our French cars to differentiate them more clearly from German models and the rest of the world's products. Going forward, it will be difficult to match Audi in the watch-like precision of its assembly techniques, yet, on the other hand, it is possible to imagine designing an interior with greater intelligence, greater originality and a fresher approach – all part of a creative upsurge conceiving genuine and often better solutions. Here is just one example: the facility to rest your leg against a door panel trimmed in shape-memory material, something that is

Stéphane Janin, long-time director of Concept Car Design at Renault.

both supple and warmly welcoming, in contrast to the type of welcome in which anything harder would be called reinforced concrete.

That would already be a first step in the quest for real and genuine comfort, comfort of the type we experience in real life rather than that portrayed in glossy brochures. And why not offer instruments on which the figures get larger or smaller depending on your speed? Or even 'intelligent' seats that provide the very best comfort for passengers by adapting themselves to longer travel itineraries such as going on holiday: not just for the first ten minutes but preferably from the third hour onwards. Equally, how about heating controls that are truly intuitive and don't force you to refer to the vehicle handbook? And the handbooks themselves have become so bulky and heavy that they fill up precious space in the glovebox - which itself often has barely enough space for anything more than gloves.

This is all part of an elaborate visual extravaganza that serves to obscure what's going on underneath, to isolate users from the mechanical realities and to develop a false impression of detached comfort. It would surely be preferable to design interiors that generate a sense of both harmony and quality - 'a leather-lined bathtub, pure and simple', as memorably described by Milen Milenovich, a highly talented designer I worked closely with for a long time and whose credits include the interior design of the Espace III.

This aspect of the move towards greater simplicity should be the real strength of a 'touch design' interior and could bring back some genuine warmth to the vehicle. This is precisely the point made by the architect Walter Gropius when he stated: 'The role of the designer is to instil a soul into the product born dead from the machine.' That's quite an undertaking.

Under my thumb

Do you remember what hi-fi sets or SLR cameras looked like in the 1970s? The more complicated they were, the better: their proud owners (who, most of the time, would not let anyone even come close to their precious possession) felt like fighter pilots or, even better, spaceship captains. They would turn knobs, fiddle with switches, scan dials, to show the rest of the world how good they were at bending complexity to their will. Now? To listen to music or to take pictures, we use our smartphones, with which our children or grandchildren are as proficient as we are (or more...). Complexity is not fashionable any more, and scores of designers constantly work on creating user-friendly devices, be it coffee makers, washing machines or cars. Still, two issues remain: the first, which Patrick le Quément's 'simplexity' addresses, is about designing beautiful user-friendliness. The second, sadly, is the tendency to keep on courting the would-be spaceship captains with cars that offer dozens of combinations of settings, as if doing the school run were akin to qualifying at the 24 Hours of Le Mans. Even worse are movement- or voice-controlled commands, which, as any dog owner knows, seldom work.

WHAT is GOOD DESIGN?

22
Concepts and Culture

The thirteenth-century Mongol leader Genghis Khan is credited with coining the motto 'Luck is the art of paying attention to the details.' It is a notion that resonates strongly with everything in our everyday lives, and it has influenced my work as a designer. What it translates into is this: if you are intent on launching a new type of vehicle onto the market, nothing should be left to chance. All expectations will be on the new vehicle to generate such a wave of excitement that its success will transform the fortunes of the company and – why not? – your own, too. For this scenario to work, absolutely everything must be examined and checked, all eventualities must be catered for, and there must be understanding and empathy for what potential customers might prefer. There is no point not going the whole way – here, good enough is no longer enough.

One of the greatest distinguishing qualities of French automobile design has been its ability to come up with new concepts that are just right for their time, either because they are tuned in to the sociocultural zeitgeist, or because they anticipate the desires and the expectations of customers. As a nation, we French have developed a strong revolutionary tradition: Fabio Filippini, former director of design at Pininfarina and who worked in France for some while, insisted to me – with some justification, though counter to generally accepted opinion – that 'in France, there is something noble about being a revolutionary.'

From the 1960s through to the 1990s France experienced a sustained wave of creativity that was encouraged by decision makers prepared to take risks in the full knowledge that, as I have stated on many occasions, failing to take the bold path might minimize the initial risk but will reduce the chances of success far more. In the post-war period this thinking helped to produce numerous models with a back-to-basics approach, such as the Citroën 2CV and the Renault 4L which, as I recall, was the first passenger car equipped with a hatchback

tailgate. Later, in much the same vein, it led to the Renault 16, which would become the first family car with a fully versatile interior. No other car has ever come close to the Citroën DS19 in the way it provided a leap into the future at a widely affordable price point, and the inimitable SM, likewise, has remained unsurpassed. The Renault 5 was the first car to feature plastic bumpers, seven years ahead of the Mercedes-Benz S-Class and, finally, the Espace opened up a whole new sector in the market: multifunctional one-box people carriers.

At the risk of being accused of nationalism, I would say that the French automobile industry has, broadly speaking, been better at innovation in the area of vehicle architectures and formats than that of any other nation. The British invented the Mini, thanks to the talented Alec Issigonis, whose origins were Greek. As for the Germans, they came up with the Messerschmitt KR175, a two-seater three-wheeler launched in 1953, though their biggest influence was the creative genius of the Porsche dynasty, the team behind the Beetle and the 911, no less. The Italians, finally, may have been outstanding stylists but they were also fortunate to count among their talents the remarkable engineer Dante Giacosa, who shaped Fiat's Topolino, and the original Multipla.

In today's fully globalized world we have to design for markets well beyond our traditional frontiers, and I don't mean just Europe but the whole world. Familiarity with our customer base is a vital element in protecting against major commercial errors: understanding our customers, their cultures, their tastes and their habits has become essential in a globalized climate that has led to a convergence of expectations. People at the same social level tend to buy the same handbags with the same logo, while others eat the same hamburgers and fries from the same polystyrene containers. And it is now vital to keep a close eye on every market so as not to repeat the mistake that was made in the 1970s, of trying

The Renault 5 (top) and the Citroën SM.

to launch a car in the United States without cup-holders. In the American value system the number of cup-holders had become a more important factor than, say, the inclusion of independent rear suspension.

For a decade or more, the Chinese market has been providing the automobile industry with the most spectacular growth it has ever experienced, and the Western automakers are all keen for a share of the cake. What a market it is – and, above all, what a culture! Chinese buyers, too, adorn themselves with handbags, umbrellas, keyrings, watches and glasses embossed with the same logos as everyone else, but there is one tradition that sets them apart from the global norm: they are superstitious. As an example of this fact, 43 per cent of Chinese people cite the figure 8 as their favourite number, as it is associated with prosperity. This means that licence plates containing the figure 8 sell for exorbitant prices and are especially highly prized by owners of Bentleys, the marque favoured by young millionaires. And did you notice that the Beijing Olympic Games opened on 8/8/2008 at 8 pm? And, to underline the special status of the figure 8, the biggest endowment made by a Chinese citizen to Harvard University amounts to – as if by chance – the sum of $8,888,888.

Chinese owners of Rolls-Royces, who tend to be older than those driving a Bentley, prefer the figure 9: it is the figure for longevity, which at some point in most people's lives becomes more important than prosperity. Likewise, it is useful to know that there is no fourth floor in Chinese hotels, apartment blocks or public buildings: the figure 4 is associated with death. Some manufacturers have had to systematically go through all their brochure materials to get rid of this figure, and it is a better idea for a model's overall length to be listed as 3.98 metres (at risk of slight distortion) rather than exactly 4 metres – unless the vehicle in question is a hearse, of course.

Cum grano salis

For car makers, innovation is a bit like salt: not enough of it, and the dish – or the car – will be bland and won't sell; too much, and it will be unpalatable, and won't sell either. Raymond Loewy, the French-born American designer, defined the right balance by the acronym MAYA, which stands for 'most advanced yet acceptable'. The problem is, how can one judge what is, or will be MAYA? Who in 1955 could have thought that the Citroën DS would become the icon of the rather conservative, still-rural, Gitanes-smoking France, and the favourite car of Charles de Gaulle, a retired general and statesman born in the nineteenth century? Conversely, why did the same French people reject such designs as the stillborn Claveau Descartes, or the clever post-war Panhards? In the UK, why was the 1930s Burney Streamline such a failure, at a time when the country featured such enlightened and far-sighted intellectuals as the Bloomsbury Group, whereas the 1959 Mini was such a hit? Studying history, culture and socio-economic trends can be useful for designers, engineers and marketing people; still, innovating remains a leap of faith. Being right at the wrong moment seldom guarantees success.

Concepts and Culture

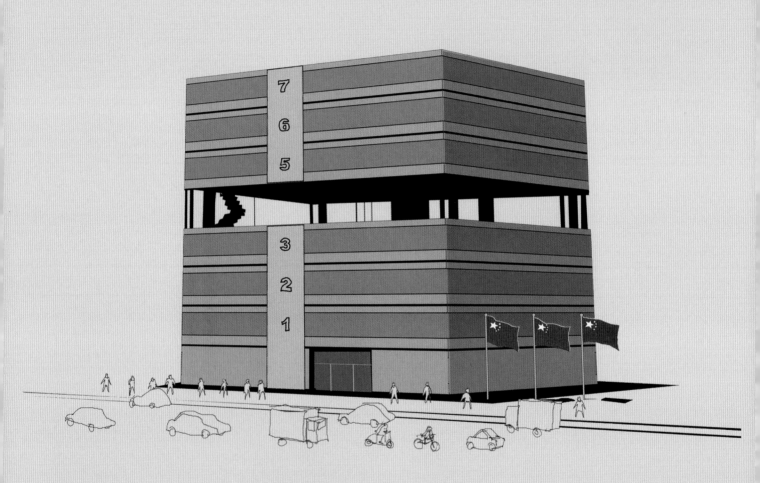

23

Thank You, Monsieur le Président

My work as a designer has brought me into contact with a significant number of company heads, chairmen and chief executives of many different nationalities and across numerous different organizations. Many of them impressed me with their strategic vision and their human qualities; in comparison, some others were almost invisible. Yet others personified the archetype of the commander, full of their own superiority and hungry for compliments. Taken as a whole, the chief executives I met were blessed with great sensitivity and were very well versed in the latest design trends. But I can remember one CEO with plenty of taste, but this time overwhelmingly poor taste, who asked for our assistance before press conferences so as to avoid making badly coordinated suit, shirt and tie choices. There was another who was painfully shy and keen to arm himself with prepared phrases to hide his awkwardness; worried about making inept remarks, he would request a private review of the design models before each of the major design selection meetings.

My first so-called presidential experience dates back to 1976, when I had only recently been appointed as director of advanced design and truck design at Ford of Europe. We had been tasked with an extremely urgent project to save a programme developed in the USA for the Brazilian market: it had gone down badly in the clinic tests there, and the whole thing had become something of a hot potato. We worked on it day and night and I flew to the US to present the project, my boss having been held back in Europe on the strategic programme that was to become the Fiesta. That is how I came to be giving my first presentation direct to God the Father, Henry Ford II, and his 'prodigal son' Lee Iacocca, the number two in the organization. Iacocca was the man behind the Mustang and who, incidentally, Mr Ford would fire in 1978, complaining that 'I don't like you...'

Bob Lutz was a remarkable president of Ford, then leader of Chrysler and, finally, at

the end of his career, at GM. A Swiss-American who, like many with his background, spoke several languages, Lutz was a distinguished and impeccably dressed figure who stood nearly 2 metres tall. A former pilot in the US Navy, he was the archetype of the American hero and, what's more, he could draw like a designer. Once, at a lunch, I surprised him as he was busy sketching on his menu the product improvements he expected to make in the wake of the presentations that morning. I offered him my own menu with this message: 'Could you please let me have your sketch when it's finished? I'd like to add you to my list of consultants.' To which he replied: 'I'm reluctant to give it to you as I've heard all about it...' Nevertheless, he did give it to me after the meal, and I still have it.

My time in Germany also brought me into close contact with the notable Carl Hahn, who presided over Volkswagen-Audi between 1982 and 1993; he was the architect of VW's success in the USA with the Beetle as well as with the Transporter van, which had been the transport of choice for the hippy generation. He hired me in 1985 with a view to becoming the first ever head of design across the whole group. His board of management included Ernst Fiala, engineering director of the Volkswagen brand, and Ferdinand Piëch, who ruled Audi with a rod of iron. Surprising though it may seem, not one of them was German: they were all Austrians. Although I had spent several years in Germany working for Ford, this was the first time I had been in an organization that was 100 per cent German. I was surprised when I saw how much passion the engineers put into their projects, and the extent to which the different brands were in permanent competition with one another to influence the choices of the broader enterprise. And I have never been involved in meetings with as much tension in the air as those between the head of Audi and the engineering director of Volkswagen.

When he arrived at Renault, future company president Louis Schweitzer – who, incidentally, was a cousin of Ford's Bob Lutz –

Left to right: Henry Ford II, Lee Iacocca, Bob Lutz, Carl Hahn, Raymond Lévy and Louis Schweitzer; the final sculpture remains unfinished.

did not have much real product experience. But he was already fired up by anything connected with design, and he later told me that his visits to Renault's Design Centre were his favourite moments during his time as president. His passion was so strong that, every time we rolled out a beautiful 1:1 scale design model for him, he always tried to get inside the vehicle. What could be more natural? Except that these hyper-realistic models never had doors that opened, and often the door handle – a dummy – would come off in his hand. In the same way, when he sat in one of our interior bucks (exact representations of a car's interior, made from foam and clay), he could never resist the temptation to shift gears, despite our warnings not to move the lever. In each of these instances remedial action in the workshop was required to get the models back into good shape, but no one resented this as it was always such a pleasure to have Schweitzer there.

Raymond Lévy, Schweitzer's predecessor, was the man who recruited me to Renault, and the company president who established design as a high-level activity, a function whose leaders could engage in intelligent discussion when called for. After my first presentation at a big design selection meeting, Lévy asked me a question. Another director, whose name I won't reveal, took it upon himself to answer in my stead because, after all, he had been to a superior elite university whose graduates were said to 'know everything, and nothing else'. Lévy shot him an angry glare and swivelled round through 90 degrees to place himself between the other director and me, the back of his head a matter of inches away from the hapless individual. Lévy then said to me: 'Monsieur le directeur du design, I asked you a question.' From then on I never experienced that kind of problem again, for the anecdote spread around the company's managers like wildfire. Merci Monsieur le président!

Civil disobedience

Designers often work according to a brief issued by their companies' CEO and inspired by said CEO's likes and dislikes, which can sometimes lead to missed opportunities, or worse. Even during the 1920s, Louis Renault considered that front brakes were hardly necessary. In the 1950s, Chrysler's K T Keller's insistence on being able to drive his cars with a hat on led to ponderous styling and low sales, until Virgil Exner finally had his say with his 1955 model range. During the 1980s, Citroën's lightweight AX had been proposed initially as a groundbreaking one-box design. The brand's top (and authoritarian) management imposed a more conventional, and ultimately dull, two-box design that did not do any justice to the AX's clever architecture. Sometimes, though, people silently resist so as to avoid imminent failures: the present author vividly remembers that the chief engineer of a major automaker carefully diluted the development costs of a very hot version of a best-selling hatch within the whole programme. Otherwise, the company's cost-killers would never have accepted the idea that this version (which was a great success in all respects) shared only 10-15 per cent common parts with its lesser siblings.

24
The Butterfly Effect

When Toyota set up its Calty Design Research centre in California in 1973, it was the first automaker of any country to establish a design operation in that American state. This, all things considered, was the most significant single move in a chain of events that would eventually lead to the disappearance of the Italian *carrozzerie* industry, showing the so-called butterfly effect in action. This is a mathematical theory popularized by the image of the single wingbeat of a butterfly in Brazil triggering a hurricane in Texas. In other words, a tiny event can have huge consequences.

Toyota's primary objective was to get closer to its largest market, the United States, and then, if possible, to establish itself in California. Throughout the 1960s and 1970s this was the US state that was ahead of the curve when it came to socio-economic and cultural trends, and it was home to a lively and dynamic creative community. But in actual fact there was another and equally important reason for Toyota's move: the Japanese manufacturer was looking for fresh influences in order to revitalize its creative forces, and it was reluctant to go to the Italian *carrozzerie* because of concerns over the vital issue of confidentiality. For Japanese producers this remains an issue of almost obsessive concern, and the example of Honda, another company known for its paranoia about secrecy, proves the point. Some while before Toyota, Honda had set up a very low-key operation in California, and it was only two years later that its presence came to light when a journalist called a phone number, obtained unofficially, and asked for the Honda Design Center. After a long silence, an Asian voice replied: 'Who gave you this number?'

In 1979 Nissan decided to establish itself in San Diego, in the extreme south of California. This was the company's first design centre outside of Japan, and now, four decades down the line, Nissan Design runs six design centres scattered around the globe. Honda officially set up in Los Angeles in 1975. One

by one, all the Japanese companies installed their research centres on the US west coast; soon the American constructors followed suit. Next to arrive were the Europeans, beginning with Volkswagen-Audi and Mercedes in 1990; BMW chose a more novel route to securing a California base when, in 1995, it bought the Designworks agency, founded by Charles (Chuck) Pelly in 1972. In the process, Chuck, who I know well, decided to take a career break and designed a very elegant catamaran, which he sailed for several months before returning to his first love and founding a new design agency, the Design Academy, in conjunction with his associate, Joan Gregor.

The Europeans had made their first move in the 1980s, establishing – albeit cautiously at first – satellite design centres based away from company headquarters, but not too far away. I was probably one of the pioneers in this regard, with the opening in 1986 of a studio in Düsseldorf for the Volkswagen Group. The motivation behind the establishment of the new creative centres was not merely to provide new sources of inspiration well away from the restrictive filtering processes of head office: it was also to breathe in the stimulating air of cities like Munich or Düsseldorf. Because, as a late-1990s advertising campaign for Monoprix reminded us, the word *ville* (city) also contains the word *vie* (life). And, at the end of the day, it was the collective desire of the design directors to shake off the practices of the recent past, which had seen the internal design operation doing little more than putting the finishing touches to projects that had originated in the Italian *carrozzerie*.

At Renault, we opened our first satellite studio in 1999 in Barcelona, under Thierry Métroz. Here, too, the main idea was to help speed up the company's stylistic evolution by bringing in fresh viewpoints from outside. This enabled the Barcelona projects to be developed in complete secrecy until the major presentations, where they were unveiled to the company's top executives. Next, we inaugurated the Paris-Bastille studio in the

A 1970s' Detroit greyman's vision of a Californian design centre.

centre of the French capital, run by the talented Fabio Filippini. Renault's acquisition of Samsung's Korean automobile operations saw Samsung Design come under the Renault umbrella the following year, and this brought about a fundamental rethink in our strategy. The role of design centres outside France would now be to work in tandem with Renault's expansion in those markets by developing projects specific to each region. Before long we had opened three more design centres: one in Bucharest in Romania, another in Mumbai, India, and the final one in São Paulo in Brazil.

The cumulative impact of the gradual opening of all these design centres by the various automakers, beginning with Toyota in California, is something that cannot be divorced from the paradigm shift that rocked the industry: manufacturers were now determined to build their own brand identities on the basis of their own strongly held internal cultural values.

In Italy, following the death of Giuseppe 'Nuccio' Bertone in 1997, his *carrozzeria* began to decline and was eventually declared insolvent in 2014; Pininfarina, for its part, was hit by a massive reduction in consultancy work from many of its automotive customers. Having lost its status, first as exclusive design consultant to Peugeot and then to other European producers, followed by the Koreans and then the Chinese, Pininfarina did not have much left. The end of its association with Ferrari, which had decided to establish its own in-house design operation, proved to be the final blow and the Indian manufacturer Mahindra & Mahindra bought the company in 2017.

The one *carrozzeria* still in reasonably good health is Italdesign, founded in 1968 by Giorgetto Giugiaro. In the wake of the 2008 financial crisis it decided to give up the struggle and in 2010 it sold 90.1 per cent of its shares to the Volkswagen Group, for a sum reputed to be 'colossal'. A few days after that sale I came to be sharing a glass of champagne with Giorgetto, who carried with him the broad smile of many great successes as well as the sadness of the memories wrapped up in them. It was then that I was reminded of the infamous butterfly effect. In truth, that evening was a sad occasion, even though the champagne was excellent.

Twist of fate

The smallest events can sometimes lead to the most important changes – or not. Sometimes, these changes are positive, and illustrate what is now called serendipity: when, in the 1940s, a chocolate bar melted in American engineer Percy Spencer's pocket as he was working on a magnetron, it ruined his trousers, but led to the invention of microwave ovens. A few years later, chocolate (again) manufacturer Pietro Ferrero went into a panic when a heatwave prevented his hazelnut *gianduja* from remaining solid, but it led to Nutella. Sometimes, the effects of these changes take a very long time to materialize: gunpowder was invented in China some time between the seventh and ninth centuries AD; however, its use in weapons became common only 600 years later. Sometimes, out of misjudgement, the consequences of a small decision can be dramatic. Car-wise, the failures in the 1960s of the Renault Dauphine and the Chevrolet Corvair in the USA were largely due to the fact that engineers had not taken into account that inflating the front and rear tyres with different pressures was too much of a hassle for the average American driver. Renault and GM lost huge sums of money; worse, the debacle led to a sizeable amount of fatalities that could have been avoided.

25

The Wheels of Modernity

I t all begins with the wheels.... Nowadays when a designer starts sketching a car, it's the wheels that appear with the first strokes of the pencil and the body comes later, but it seems that this has not always been the case. Before the advent of design schools such as ArtCenter in Pasadena, California, in 1930 or even France's Strate School of Design in 1993, the process would begin with a number of drawings, without wheels; the wheels would be added only in the final version. The ArtCenter (the first school to teach what at the time was known as automobile styling) and Strate stress the importance of a complete mastery of drawing as an essential qualification for any car designer. It should be pointed out that sketching a wheel is no easy task, as it requires proficiency in the art of perspective drawing. I have often reflected that in their day my predecessors must have tackled this chore with some reluctance and a lump in the throat. In my office I still have a beautiful painting of a Gordini – without wheels. Or maybe they are there, but tucked in so carefully that they cannot be seen, as if they had been incarcerated in wheelarches that have turned into prison cells?

A car wheel: what precisely is it? A tyre, a rim... and a lot of style. And the size of the wheels is one of the obsessions shared by every designer in the world. It is counted a major triumph to convince top company managers to launch a new car fitted with a larger wheel size than that on the outgoing model. Whenever a new model comes up for review, a message along the lines of 'we will be offering an option of 19-inch or even 20-inch wheels' is signal of success. And this is why Renault pushed this to an extreme by offering the 2016 Scénic with 20-inch wheels across the board. Of course width is important, too, and for a long time this was the most important factor; today, although width is still a symbol of power, it also stands for an era that has passed.

It took some time before the wheels became smoothly integrated within the overall design of cars. The very first cars were a confection, whether visually coherent or not, of a set of disparate components: bonnet, windscreen, mudguards, doors, running boards and, of course, wheels. To these were added all the accessories, such as headlights, sidelights and horns, just like glitterball decorations on a Christmas tree. The end result was a mobile machine with, for the most part, about as much charm as a lawnmower. The mudguards gradually lost their separate status and eventually merged with the main body to form an integrated pontoon that was a single form rather than a collection of unrelated elements. Pininfarina was one of the first to design car bodies in this manner, first of all in the 1930s with the Lancia Aprilia coupé and, most importantly, the Cisitalia 202, the car that changed automotive style in the post-1945 period. And the wheels, swept up in the same trend to become part of a coherent whole, were pushed outwards to finish flush with the bodywork and thus fill almost the entire wheelarch.

The post-war years witnessed the blossoming of a uniquely French speciality: small wheels, hidden behind aerodynamic add-ons, as on the DS, or the 1964 Panhard CD prototype, where the front wheels were faired in as well as the rears. Those were the years when our ingenious French engineers were fanatical in their pursuit of aerodynamic efficiency, of lightness and of fuel economy. Indeed, the organizers of the 24 Hours of Le Mans race invented a special category – the famous Index of Performance classification – within the race rules so as to allow these tiny 'mosquitoes on wheels' to compete for prizes. Throughout this period the German manufacturers were majoring on power, with big wheels shoehorned into their arches – larger, more outward, more extrovert.

Yet we in France were not the only ones to fit wheels that were undersize and set too far in from the body sides. Take a British example: the Jaguar E-Type, one of the most beautiful cars ever produced by that giant of style, Sir William Lyons. Whatever our English friends

Two very different approaches in racing cars: the enormously powerful Porsche 917 of 1969 (left), and the lightweight Panhard CD LM64 (far left) with exceptionally fine-tuned aerodynamics resulting in very low consumption.

might say, the positioning of the wheels on this car is, quite simply, a visual disaster. Where are they? Where have the wheels gone? It's intriguing to compare the E-Type, launched in 1961, with a Ferrari 250GT of 1960: the latter displays perfect visual harmony between its body and chassis and sits very comfortably on its wheels. There's simply no comparison.

Looking closely at the fabulous cars gathered together for the most recent *concours d'élégance* at Villa d'Este (see page 192), I was reminded of the thoughts put forward by a former director of the Italian *carrozzeria* Pininfarina. He explained to me why, before World War II, his rival coachbuilder, Touring, had always been able to produce cars that were more beautiful to look at than his own. The explanation was very clear: while Touring shaped its bodies almost exclusively for Alfa Romeo, which was well known for having chassis with wide tracks front and rear, Pininfarina was associated mainly with the Lancia marque, which tended to be less generous in this regard. Alfa Romeo is still thriving, but the Lancia marque has all but disappeared. Which just goes to show...

The wheels of fortune

Forget printing, steam, or the internet: the most important technological breakthrough in the history of mankind was made 4000 or 5000 years ago, and it was the wheel. The wheel can drag objects as well as move them. It can accelerate or slow movement, and it absorbs obstacles and reduces effort. The wheel is so essential that it actually is at the heart of automotive design. On Tutankhamun's chariot, wheels were already covered in electrum, an alloy of gold and silver, and played a major part in the appeal of the Pharaoh's carriage: they symbolized speed, beauty and power. They remain a key feature of iconic cars today: it is very difficult to imagine a classic Porsche 911 without its five-spoke Fuchs alloys, a Ferrari 250 GT SWB without its glistening Borrani wires, or even a VW Beetle without its bowl-shaped hubcaps. Wheels remain a crucial issue for today's designers, but the growing obsession for ever-larger diameters is not without problems: comfort, aerodynamic drag and unsprung weight seem to be overlooked for elegance's sake. Filling the wheel arches is a respectable ambition, but function seems sacrificed to form. Which seems rather paradoxical, for what remains the most functional of objects.

The Wheels of Modernity

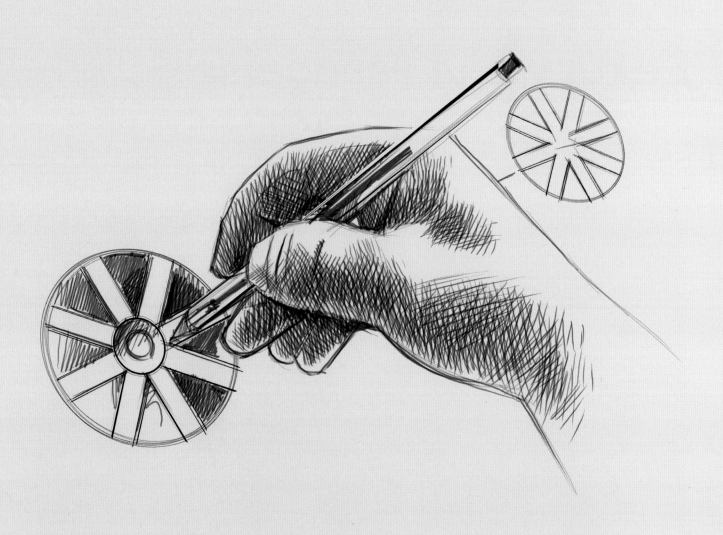

26
Luxury à la Française

In 1992 I had the honour of being asked to preside over the jury for the European Design Awards for that year. In my preface for the booklet drawn up for the competition I posed the following questions: 'In the future, what will become of the French or Italian characteristics that today define us? And how will it be possible to remain German while at the same time being European?' The questions prompted vigorous discussion among my colleagues, and the debate became even more animated after I had taken the opportunity to throw in a quotation from the French president Charles de Gaulle from 1962: 'Dante, Goethe and Chateaubriand belong to the whole of Europe insofar as they were so typically Italian, German and French, respectively.' Some twenty-five years since that design competition and more than fifty since de Gaulle's declaration, where are we on this now? It is clear that national designs have all but disappeared, replaced by an international design language that some have described as 'one size fits all' and in which no one questions the dominance of German influence. *Deutsches Design über alles* ('above all')?

It wasn't always thus. In the period before World War II France was by far the most influential nation when it came to the art of automobile design, with *carrosseries* such as Chapron, Pourtout, Labourdette, Franay and Letourneur & Marchand. French style also inspired designers from outside France; witness the fabulous creations of Howard 'Dutch' Darrin (an American), Jacques Saoutchik (born in modern-day Belarus) and Giuseppe Figoni (Italian), all of whom were very strongly influenced by the art deco movement. Another distinct characteristic of French style is lightness, something that was so important to the structural engineer Gustave Eiffel and which found its expression in the pencil strokes of an Italian automobile designer, Ettore Bugatti, and his son Jean. The automobile did no more than reflect what was going on in the world of fine art, with the École de Paris movement counting among its ranks

Pablo Picasso, Chaim Soutine, Marc Chagall, Alexander Archipenko and Amedeo Modigliani.

Having had the good fortune in my own career to have worked in teams nearly always made up of designers of many nationalities, I have always been impressed by the open-mindedness that multiculturalism brings to those teams. And with certain non-French designers I could even sense that there was a heightened awareness of the unique qualities that go to make up the 'French touch' (see page 93), precisely because those individuals had come from elsewhere and had known other cultures. A bit like the man who is walking along the banks of a river during a heatwave and feels the urge to dive into the clear water. He sees a fish and asks it: 'Hey, little fish, please tell me, what's the water like?' To which the fish replies: 'Water? What water?'

After the war, everything had changed: *Vae victis* (Latin for 'woe to the conquered'). Industrially, the expression could have been applied to the growing influence of America, with its wings and fins, its chrome, its bright colours and brash ornamentation – not just in the USA itself but also in Germany, in France (remember the Simca Vedette Versailles and Chambord?) and elsewhere too. Thank goodness, we were able to turn the page on that one pretty quickly and move on to the next chapter – *grazia*, or grace. This found its expression in the work of Italian *carrozzerie* like the Tourings and the Pininfarinas.

So, after the temptation of the transatlantic, French constructors then indulged en masse in their cooperation with the Italian coachbuilders – and it was only later, towards the end of the 1980s and after having been stung by the realization that our friends from across the Alps had been offering their customers too many designs that were very similar, that the French constructors were able to regain their cultural independence. The 1960s 'cloning' between the Peugeot 404, Austin Cambridge and Lancia Flaminia (see page 61) was perhaps the most blatant, but it was not an isolated example. Working for one

The Franco-British Concorde supersonic passenger airliner, in its day the symbol of luxurious travel, above the Renault Initiale concept car.

major manufacturer, I saw with my own eyes a coachbuilder's design model that had already been rejected by my previous company.

It is now more than twenty-five years since automakers began to regain control of their destinies by creating powerful in-house design centres. But have these centres helped companies to restore their creative autonomy? There's not much to suggest they have – but why not? Because of a lack of talent? Absolutely not. The burden of history? A bit, no doubt. Like it or not, car design filters downwards from the high-end models, and the German automakers are the only ones to have established and developed a credible presence in this market in the post-war period. In France our priorities were to focus our efforts on vehicles that were efficient and intelligent, but at the lower end of the market; French manufacturers continue to miss opportunities for genuinely high-end models. All the foreign designers that I have had the pleasure of working with have expressed their incredulity when it comes to this: why is France, the premier nation for fashion and luxury, still incapable of delivering these values in the domain of the automobile?

For sure, there have been some attempts. Forgive me for preaching my own sermon, but one of the most pertinent attempts was Renault's Initiale concept car, presented at the 1995 Frankfurt motor show and a project that very nearly became a production reality. Sadly, the project was stopped partway through its development as it was judged to be too ambitious: it was dropped in favour of another concept that, though intelligent, suffered from awkward proportions.

In the 1970s Yves Georges, then head of Renault's engineering division, would have reliably reminded everyone that the role of styling was to 'dress up the hunchback – what a programme...!' But in spite of all our efforts, Renault Design and the Initiale lost the battle and the Vel Satis got the decision. Once again, we should have contested this: often, an innovation is a transgression that succeeds. And this, regrettably, is how luxury *à la française* came to be buried for two generations or more.

Globetrotters

What car could be more quintessentially British than an Aston Martin DB4? More Germanic than a 'Heckflosse' (fintail) Mercedes 220? More innovatively Gallic than a Citroën DS? Yet the Aston and the Citroën were designed by Italians, and the Mercedes by a Frenchman. Does this mean that, even in the 1960s, globalization was already looming? Actually, not quite. Car design has always been international, even if France initially led the race. In the era of horse carriages, French coachbuilders reigned, and some of them – in the same way Hooper did in Britain – successfully switched to horseless carriages. During the 1930s, every reputable designer of whatever country had to spend time in France, to the extent that two Americans, Tom Hibbard and Howard Darrin, decided to stay and open a French *carrosserie*. Paris was the capital city of coachbuilding, but it was a cosmopolitan city in that respect too: Jacques Saoutchik was born in Belarus, Jean Antem was Spanish, Giuseppe Figoni and Ovidio Falaschi were Italian. And this had already been the case when the French *carrosseries* that started working on cars comprised Kellner, Kelsch and Mühlbacher, all founded by German and Austrian immigrants.

27

Greenhouse on the Move

English-speaking automotive design professionals have their own highly specialized vocabulary, something reminiscent of a secret society's language. In this designer code the passenger compartment is known as a glasshouse or greenhouse. In the late 1970s, when I was at Ford, the Sierra programme was regarded by Henry Ford II as too futuristic. To defend the programme, we at Ford Design undertook a study called 'Greenhouse on the Move', in which we looked back at the history of the automobile so as to trace the evolution of the glazed areas of the vehicle (windscreen, side windows, rear window).

At the end of the 1920s and in the early 1930s automotive beauty found its expression in long bonnets and a short passenger cabin, pushed towards the rear; the wheels were set at the four corners and overhang front and rear were kept to a minimum. The whole aesthetic shouted out speed and power, with an engine compartment as long as a station platform. This is seen in large and grandiose limousines such as the ultra-luxurious Bugatti Type 41 Royale 'Coupé Napoléon', launched in 1929, and the remarkable Bucciali TAV 8-32 of 1931, designed by Jacques Saoutchik and complete with a V12 Voisin engine and wheels more than a metre in diameter. These were the glory years of the great French *carrossiers* and long bonnets were the order of the day. Some designs even featured fairings covering the rear wheels, giving the whole ensemble the feeling of a sculpture shimmering above the ground. But once the automobile had become a generalized means of transport the passenger cabin began to grow in volume and, as it was unable to expand rearwards, it started to move towards the font, pushing the windscreen forward in the process.

After World War II, the automotive landscape had changed, in France just as everywhere else in Europe. Now the priority was to democratize car ownership and to offer compact models with enough space for four or five people. The portion given over to passenger accommodation became the dominant influence on the overall architecture of the vehicle, whether it was equipped with front-wheel drive (as in the brilliant Citroën 2CV) or was rear-engined like the Renault 4CV. The rear-wheel drive option, which stemmed from the Volkswagen Beetle, was the favoured solution for several years and even served to keep cement works happy: in winter, and at other times, too, carrying a sack of cement in the front luggage compartment helped drivers to avoid losing control.

The arrival of the Mini in 1959 instantly rewrote the rules of the game. Now the passenger cabin expanded decisively forward to take up two-thirds of the car's overall length. Until that point the British manufacturers had failed to contribute much to the advancement of automobile architecture, but now, in a single move, they gained a major advantage in the compactness of the mechanical elements and thus in maximizing the interior space on offer. After the Mini, everything was different. In a flash, such companies as Peugeot, Opel and Ford, who had failed to invest in front-wheel drive, found their small- and medium-car ranges out of date. Even the German premium manufacturers, faithful to the traditional engineering template of front engine and rear-wheel drive, were getting worried as front-drive designs were much better when it came to handling and roadholding – even though their Achilles heel was transmitting high levels of torque through the front wheels.

Over the course of my years at Ford I worked on numerous projects based on platforms that were sadly out of date. On each occasion we had to mimic the appearance of a front-drive car, even though our cars were often as outmoded as a carriage with an engine strapped on. Eventually the whole world went over to front-wheel drive, apart from the German premium manufacturers (except Audi). And, as time passed, technology and driving aids began to allow rear-drive cars to deal with their handicaps, and then to overcome them before once again becoming the yardstick for handling.

The Bucciali TAV 8-32.

The forward march of the passenger compartment was to experience two last pushes. To everyone's surprise, the first came from Chrysler at the 1992 Detroit show when it launched the 1993 Vision, based on the front-wheel drive LH platform. The windscreen was pushed further forward than had ever been seen before, in accordance with the new 'Cab Forward' design philosophy. The dash top was so deep that it was impossible to get a pair of sunglasses back if you'd had to brake suddenly. And of course there was the Renault Espace and its competitors, which had provided the inspiration for the Chrysler. For a long while, in fact, and before the SUVs wiped them out, much like hornets kill bees, the one-box Espace-type vehicle was believed by many to represent the ultimate goal in the automobile revolution. But that was yesterday.

Yet, today, in your opinion, which design provides the best expression of the quintessence of automobile art? Without a moment's hesitation I would say the BMW 4-Series coupé: an ultra-short front overhang, a long bonnet and a steeply raked windscreen combine to produce great elegance. Do you get the feeling you've read this description somewhere before? If so, reread the second paragraph: the BMW represents a spectacular return to the values of yesteryear. Which goes to show that, to come back into fashion, all you have to do is simply wait long enough.

All in front

In traditional horse-drawn carriages the driver generally sat right at the front, although there were a few exceptions – among which the British hansom cab stands out. However, horses, and thus horse-power, always remained out in front. Does that mean that the aesthetic tradition of long bonnets is linked to the fact that these bonnets do contain 'horsepower'? Maybe, even notwithstanding any psychoanalytic references to phallic representations of power. In any event, designers who try to maximize passenger and luggage space, and to minimize space taken up by the engine, are always regarded with some suspicion. Of course, the Mini has become a universal standard of space efficiency, but before it, the American Dymaxion by the architect and inventor Buckminster Fuller and the Scarab by US aviation engineer William Stout, to name just two, had been resounding failures. Meanwhile, even the humble and clever Citroën 2CV boasted a bonnet that was totally out of proportion to its tiny flat-twin engine. And for a time, the success of one-box MPVs such as the Renault Espace or the Toyota Previa provided hope that interior space was becoming an overriding priority. Even so, the need for uselessly but beautifully long bonnets seems to have come back for good: Tesla Model S, anyone?

28
Avantime... Out of Time

After the third-generation Espace was launched in 1996, Renault president Louis Schweitzer informed the senior management of Matra, which produced the car, that this would be the last model to be manufactured at their Romorantin plant and that the next generation of the Espace would be made from sheet metal so that it could be produced in one of Renault's own factories from 2002.

The original 1984 Espace monospace, or one-box people carrier, was conceived by the very gifted automotive engineer Philippe Guédon, head of Matra; the vehicle's versatile modular interior would be Renault's contribution to the project. Jacques Cheinisse, Renault's product planning director in charge of high-end vehicles, had been greatly impressed by the potential of the project at a preliminary presentation, and arranged for Matra to present its P23 concept to senior Renault management in late 1982. Opening the meeting, Cheinisse declared: 'As soon as we saw the bottle, we realized that we could apply our own ideas to the interior.' And as the meeting ended, Bernard Hanon, Renault's president at the time, delivered an assessment that would come to be famous: 'This is the vehicle people will naturally graduate to once they have got past all the stages of automotive ego.' But those comments could not have anticipated the Avantime, some twenty years later, nor the fact that, sadly, the progress of history is rarely linear.

The Espace was a massive success and established a totally new segment in the car market, but so strong was the demand for the model that it outstripped the capacity of Matra's factory. The plant was equipped to build vehicles with bodies made from composite materials, a technique until then reserved for small production runs and thus poorly suited to the bigger volumes being generated by the Espace's success with customers in Europe.

Matra was freed from its exclusive contract with Renault and encouraged to seek other partners, something it tried to do but without success. First off, Matra proposed to Renault a concept that turned out to be a clever, though flawed, idea: an ultra-compact vehicle in which the rear occupants faced backwards. Next, Matra's designers came up with another completely new idea, a 'coupé space'. Philippe Guédon explained that the buyer group could be former Espace owners whose families had grown up, but who still wanted to retain the high driving position and unmatched all-round vision. This became the Avantime, an entirely new species and the first-ever crossover, its mission being to answer to those looking for a car for pleasure.

The Avantime was designed by the very imaginative Thierry Métroz at Renault immediately after he had completed the fourth-generation Espace. We took our inspiration from the Vel Satis concept car shaped by Florian Thiercelin for Renault's centenary in 1998; this should not be confused with the production sedan of the same name that came out in 2002, but which had very few design cues in common with the concept. The Vel Satis concept car was in essence a one-box coupé, low to the ground and very luxurious, and with a rear-end design that introduced the vertical semicircular rear window that was later picked up on the Mégane II and Scénic II, as well as the Avantime and Espace IV.

The Avantime project was based on the platform of the Espace III, while the Espace IV was to employ an all-new architecture for upper-segment vehicles, tied in with new engines. The Avantime was equipped with two massive pantograph side doors, the idea being to provide easy access to the rear seats and also to simplify exit in confined parking spaces. To achieve this, Matra came up with the idea of doors with double-jointed hinges, which was easy enough to achieve on a one-off concept car prototype that was never out of the sight of the technicians and fixers that accompanied it. But with the production car it proved to be a different matter. It was a quasi-impossible mission to

The Avantime.

An image of destruction, of the end of a factory that for many years had produced all the Matra cars.

perfect those doors, and all the other complex associated issues, so as to provide the smooth functionality and perceived quality that are de rigueur for top-of-the-line products. For me this was a very difficult period as between 1995 and 1999 I was in charge of both design and quality. This meant I was torn between my conscience as head of group-wide quality, which told me I must not release a project onto the market before it was fully developed, and my sensibilities as a designer who was aware of the danger that any further delays risked making a fresh product seem stale and also overexposed. The Avantime was eventually launched in 2001, more than a year late and with just a single engine option, a three-litre petrol V6. 'Avantime, out of time' turned the whole of our planned large-car strategy upside down – it was a disaster.

The underlying problem at Matra was its inability to secure any contracts beyond the one with Renault for the Avantime. This solitary small-series project did not provide enough volume to keep Matra profitable: for that, at least two more programmes would have been needed. As a result, Matra was losing a lot of money on a daily basis and, unable to find a way out, the parent organization, the Lagardère Group, took the decision to close the plant.

So that is how the Avantime came to make a premature exit, off the market and into the history books just three years after its launch. The model itself deserved much better; a factory was closed, thousands of people were put on the dole and a whole region was suffocated. What a mess....

Yet, even today, when I meet automotive journalists of any nationality, two models regularly crop up: Twingo and Avantime, both of them for their concept as well as for their stylistic impact. These models, so the journalists maintain, represent 'the French touch' in car design, and they add that 'only the French could have produced cars like that.'

Vanitas vanitatum

Cars are means of transport, but whatever the era, means of transport have also been, and remain, symbols of social status. If not, why would there be several classes in trains, planes or boats? Still, all through the history of cars, automakers have tried, sometimes successfully, to sell 'no-frills' cars, which simply served the purpose of getting as cheaply and as efficiently as possible from A to B. Actually, two of them are among the all-time best-sellers (the Model-T Ford and the VW Beetle), and some of them have had the longest lifespan: the VW Beetle again, the original Land Rover (later known as the Defender), the 2CV, the Renault 4. However, things get more complicated when the idea is to produce a middle- or upper-class car with the same aim: the more expensive the car, the less its customers want it to be useful. Rover's spacious, ergonomic and modern 1976 SD1 was considered to be too austere until its wonderful dashboard was spoilt by lashings of wood. Likewise, MPVs have vanished, to be replaced by SUVs: the pretence of an adventurous lifestyle probably matters to drivers who would rather be taken for rugged adventurers than for dads and mums going to the supermarket.

29

Choosing: It's as Much About Electing as Excluding

Choosing one design model from a selection of proposals is no easy matter, especially as a multitude of engineering or financial factors can influence the choice. And sometimes internal politics can also manifest themselves as a rogue, though all too real, element.

It all begins with the decision to replace an existing model, to open up a new segment in the market, or to enter a sector where the brand has been absent until now. First come surveys of market trends and sociocultural analyses. These are followed by an advanced research phase during which several different architectural alternatives are pitched against one another to decide on a single solution to pursue. It is at this point that the real design competition starts; this is zero, and the finish line is at 100 – but it isn't about acceleration. Instead, the context is the process that leads to a final selection: the presentation of the design brief (which includes the vehicle's architecture) to all the designers, and the review by the director of design of about a hundred sketches.

But then the question arises: how do you whittle a hundred ideas down to a dozen? The early twentieth-century French novelist André Gide explained it as 'choosing being as much about electing as excluding'. Each time I had to make this type of selection I asked my teams to keep the number of proposals to a figure that allowed for sensible human discussion, but without provoking any undue anxiety.

The process having been kicked off with the sketches and package drawings, most companies then move to matching each of the designers with a digital modeller; these pairings develop around a dozen proposals that can be projected onto a giant screen, or powerwall, more than 6 metres long and 2.5 metres tall. This can display the virtual model from every angle and can zoom in on details – but that's not all. The top design centres have developed digital film techniques that allow the virtual model to be dropped into different environments to see how its look

changes in, say, an urban setting, a Californian freeway or a forest track.

Thanks to the widespread availability of digital film techniques, the evaluation of design proposals has improved dramatically: we have moved from a purely static (and therefore very restricted) assessment to being able to view the model in action. In this sense the automobile has at last come to replace the auto*immobile*.

The next step sees the production of about ten fullsize models in expanded polystyrene: these allow a better appreciation of the proportions of each one and enable a further selection until only five or six remain. After some weeks of fine-tuning, the decision is made to mill five or six fullsize models in hard foam. These will later be prepared and painted so they look hyper-realistic at the big theme selection meeting. Those attending will include senior company vice-presidents representing the major divisions – product planning, marketing, engineering, finance and design – who select the two proposals that will then be candidates when the final choice is made.

By the time the big day finally arrives, the two models that have gone through have been refined with great precision, sculpted using a special clay. Occasionally the models are moulded in glass fibre to provide a finish so realistic that at the end of the session it is necessary to collect up all the dummy door handles that have been pulled off. The design of the interior progresses in parallel, with up to five instrument panel bucks presented, and the two best ones go through to the final round (often called the 'Go With One' decision), to select the preferred exterior and interior themes.

These product selection meetings are always grand occasions, usually memorable for better or for worse; they can often be exciting, but occasionally they can turn into a bit of a scrum. Every now and then I even got the feeling that I had been drawn into a re-enactment of the court of Louis XIV.

Design: Between the Lines

I have also been involved in selection sessions where there were too many proposals to choose from, as with one for a Ford Escort that I will never forget. All the proposals were so similar, almost down to the last detail, that one of the directors, who had already spent some time reviewing the models in a preliminary briefing, was moved to ask: 'Now, which is the one that we all liked?'

And then there was a ridiculous instance that came at the time when the Italian domination of the style business was at its height. The product planning director of a major French marque, who had a reputation for regularly being late for important company meetings, arrived some time after the product selection meeting had started. So as not to appear out of the loop, he asked: 'Which is the proposal from our favourite Italian design house?' The deputy design director, Jacques Nocher, pointed towards a model and the product planning director, great aesthete that he was, immediately exclaimed: 'What sensuality! His proportions are truly fabulous – you can tell right away that it was designed by the *Maestro* himself.' Hearing these words, Nocher changed his mind and said that he had made a mistake: the model he had pointed out had been produced in-house. The proposal by the *Maestro* was the one right next to it. The insolent Nocher was rebuked, and when the time came the product director voted for the model from the *Maestro*.

My last boss at Renault, Carlos Ghosn, asked me shortly after his arrival to reorganize these product selection meetings so as to eliminate this type of behaviour. As a result, my executive secretary, Jean-Marie Souquet, suggested that each person taking part in these sessions should fill out an assessment form for each proposal being considered, stating his or her choice in front of the committee and without any consultation with other members. Playtime's over!

Camels, horses and dictators

The design community credits Alec Issigonis for stating that 'a camel is a horse designed by a committee'. Whether he originated that famous line or not, it faithfully reflects the self-confidence the Mini's creator showed all his life. It is also, unfortunately, often true. As creative as they are, designers sometimes have to yield to people who are higher on the corporate ladder, and to come up with aesthetic compromises that will satisfy the powers that be. Worse still, however, is dictatorial design, when decisions are taken by someone who is in charge but does not really have the necessary knowledge to make the right choices. Exceptions do exist, of course: Jaguar's William Lyons, himself no mean designer, never signed off an ugly car. And no one would have dared to criticize Citroën's Flaminio Bertoni's proposals. Still, exceptions are exceptions. And even the most enlightened dictators can make mistakes: the Jaguar Mark X was a commercial failure, and Flaminio Bertoni designed not only the DS, but also, unfortunately, the Ami 6, whereas such committee-designed cars as the 1962 Ford Cortina and the 1966 Chevrolet Camaro actually were nice cars in every respect.

Choosing: It's as Much About Electing as Excluding

30

Who's in the Details?
God or the Devil?

'The devil is in the detail.' So goes the familiar saying, generally attributed to the nineteenth-century German philosopher Friedrich Nietzsche, and in common use in both Germany and the English-speaking world. It's a maxim that, though ambiguous, is taken to mean that the details should never be neglected as they can have a diabolical effect on the whole. Several decades later the architect and designer Ludwig Mies van der Rohe, a German who became a naturalized American, took up the slogan 'God is in the details.' His message was the opposite: that it is only by virtue of the quality of its details that a work can be considered complete and beautiful. But how do these oh-so-serious philosophical questions relate to car design? Be patient, and don't turn the page – I'm getting there!

When the conversation turns to elegant and collectable cars of the 1950s, the talk is invariably about their skilfully balanced proportions, their sweeping lines, their wheels set flush to the body sides, the distinctive shapes of their radiator grilles. What is almost never touched upon, however, is the design of their headlights, sidelights and tail lights. For many decades the automobile industry was held back by the companies that supplied lighting: headlamps were of various sizes, but exclusively round, something that relegated them to the list of sundry details that could not usefully contribute towards the vehicle's overall appearance. Later, the first examples of rectangular headlights appeared, initially on the 1960 Ford Taunus and then on the Citroën Ami 6 – even if that car relied more on its reverse-raked rear window, borrowed from the Ford Anglia, to define its character.

Throughout most of the 1970s, constructors remained resigned to fitting the standard off-the-shelf headlights imposed on them by suppliers intent on maximizing their economies of scale; later, the automakers were able to break out of this straightjacket and develop headlamp designs specific to each of their models and shaped to blend in with the front-end styling. What freedom! What a luxury! Next, clear headlamp lenses in polycarbonate began to take over from glass, allowing designers to get away from the old optical ribbing: clear lenses immediately became a sign of modernity.

Sadly, however, this technology arrived too late to be included in the design of the Renault Clio II, under development in 1998. It could almost certainly have been possible to build in this feature, but that would have made the completion of the programme more complex and, regrettably, we were unable to make the programme leader recognize how this small detail could have promoted our new car into the ranks of 'very nearly modern' models. It must be said that this brilliant engineer never focused on the latest trends or the mood of the moment. (And incidentally, he rationalized his wardrobe into two sections, one for summer and the other for winter, the switchover taking as its cue the firing up of the communal central heating system in his building.) Too bad!

In the end, we had to wait until the Clio's facelift in 2001 before we adopted smooth headlight lenses like everyone else. Admittedly, though, at the time headlights had not yet become the signature feature of a model's stylistic image. I would also note that in the 1950s that most prolific of Italian designers, Giovanni Michelotti, presented no fewer than fifty design studies at the 1953 Turin motor show. If he had had to design all the headlights, sidelights and tail lights specifically for each model, his productivity would have fallen dramatically – to the detriment of the history of the automobile.

Today, headlights and front and rear lighting are no longer treated as mere details; instead, they are an essential part of the model's light signature, no less. That's a million miles away from the situation when I first started in this profession, when the design of lighting was the responsibility of so-called 'senior' designers, most of them of the pipe-and-slippers generation and who at the end of a long career tended to favour the easy way out. Nowadays this work is entrusted to special teams of young and passionate designers, often with backgrounds in graphics and often locked in something of a power struggle with 'traditional' designers. I'm thinking of those working in the areas of exterior and interior design and colour and trim, all of whom want to dazzle us with their brilliance and earn their place in the limelight.

That is how we have come to progress gradually from frontal identities revolving first and foremost around a grille and its logo, to a fresh approach that underlines the identity of the brand even more powerfully. The starting point here is the positioning of the headlights, with their carefully shaped profiles – only for those carefully drawn shapes later to virtually disappear in the dark as they became outshone by the light signature. The origins of this additional light signature trace back to an idea from Scandinavia that had the aim of saving many lives. So now the new 'light signature' designers can thank the European rule makers for their inspiration. I imagine that at every automaker and in every lighting

design section they must have set up an altar and lit a candle in honour of their great champion, LED lighting.

But what have our young and ambitious designers done since then? First off, they got us accustomed to these highly efficient signalling lights but kept them discreet. And then they turned the lights into the equivalent of a mini Las Vegas by night, something that makes me think of the intricate baroque chrome decorations American designers applied to their cars in the late 1950s, for example the 1959 Oldsmobile Ninety-Eight.

My experience tells me that such excesses are always transitory. They will be followed by a period of greater maturity when things will be more in proportion. And even though everything will obviously be different, we will still return to the principle that, in any composition, the sum total of the details constitutes the whole. Which reminds me of this delightful reflection from Antoine de Saint-Exupéry, author of *The Little Prince* (1943): 'Perfection is achieved not when there is nothing left to add, but when there is nothing left to take away.'

Let there be light

Like eyes, car lights have a dual purpose: on the one hand they are the instruments through which we can see; on the other, they are also a key to seduction, since cars almost always have a 'face'. Even before LEDs, xenon and electronics, making lights more efficient was a key issue for car makers, as shown by Cadillac's 1950s Autronic eye and GM's 1960 Twilight Sentinel, which provided automatic dimming, or by the Citroën DS and SM directional lights. Manufacturers have always sought to make lights more attractive, too: even the arch-conventional Lucas P100 headlight was as ornate as a silversmith's work, and sequential rear lights, which first appeared in the Ford Thunderbird, were all the rage in the USA for quite a long time. However, the present times are, in this domain as in many others, paradoxical: lights have become incredibly efficient, providing a powerful lighting that automatically adjusts to any oncoming traffic, but in Western countries few people ever drive at night on unlit roads any more. Lights have also become so compact that integrating them into a front design has never been easier. Still, we are definitely not prepared to accept cars that look blind. We can do without grilles. But lights?

Who's in the Details? God or the Devil?

31

Those Mickey Mouse Ears

Around the world, a large number of industrial designers – and an even greater number of architects – are entirely ignorant of one of the best-kept secrets in car design. And because they are not in the know, they keep on designing and putting into production by the tens of thousands or sometimes millions, products that suffer from a clear and very basic defect. Yet, over the course of almost fifty years, nothing has really changed. How can we tolerate a scandal on this scale?

This secret has to this day remained so closely guarded that whenever someone initiated into the car design world breaches the unspoken ethical code that the profession upholds – for example by designing a product other than a vehicle – it is usually done on the quiet, as if it were an illicit venture. Yet, as a car designer myself, I can immediately tell whether a particular object has passed through the hands of an automotive designer: if it has, the shapes that make up the product are generally much more fluid.

For my part I first discovered the 'Mickey Mouse ears' phenomenon not as a visitor to one of Disney's theme parks but in the mid-1970s at the Ford Design Centre in Germany, in the context of a fullsize line draft. As in most design centres at the time, there was a huge workshop where full-scale design models were being worked on in a special clay that has the characteristic of being malleable when warm, but which hardens when it cools. In one corner of the vast studio was a 6-metre-long table; remembering that in those days all car-body design was drawn by hand and at full scale, this meant that the design draughtspeople had to spend part of their day stretched out full-length on that big table. Their work consisted of using French curves to link and extend lines, which required them to view the results of their efforts from an angle of 30 degrees.

As it happens, it was here that I met my first 'magician' of the fullsize line-drafting process, Mike Painter. Mike was an Englishman who spoke German with such a thick accent that to start with I needed the services of an interpreter to understand him, even though I could already speak German; he was the first person to explain to me exactly what the secret of 'Mickey Mouse ears' was.

Now what I am about to tell you will change the way you look at mass-produced objects, and you will become one of the initiates who may, just as an example, go on to scrutinize a smartphone screen with an educated eye. The secret is quite simple: any rectangle or square looks perfect when viewed square on. Yet if the four corners are radiused, you'll notice that these radii appear to bulge out of the frame and give an impression of incompatibility. In order to correct this optical illusion, you have to take the radii at each corner and ease them inwards along their centre line; next, you link these radii to the straight sides with a gentle curve to soften the transition into the arc, just as shown in the illustration on page 135.

Things get even more complicated when it comes to a 3D sculpted volume. Here, the challenge is to channel the trajectory of light so that its path across the surface is uninterrupted; everything needs to be done with real subtlety as it is a question of mere millimetres. These areas of transition are often poorly handled by non-automotive designers, and also by engineers who are content with simply adding a radius to join tangential surfaces together. A skilled automotive design draughtsperson would push that tangency a little further outwards, towards what is known as the continuity of transition. In truth, all this takes place within these few tiny millimetres of transition.

The amount of light reflected back from a surface depends directly on the size of the object's radius: if there is not a smooth transition into the radius the result is a discontinuity in the highlight, which can then look like an uncontrolled imperfection. Some may insist that this is no more than a detail but, as the great twentieth-century American designer Charles Eames said, 'the details are not the details. They make the product.'

Fast forward to 2010 when I kicked off my new life in the world of yachting: I began by designing a first sailing vessel in conjunction with the team of highly accomplished naval architects from VPLP. What I brought along was my knowledge of shapes and forms and the many techniques associated with them, including the famous 'Mickey Mouse ears', techniques I had already introduced into the culture of Renault Design. (As an aside, those ideas had been taken on board by all the designers who had been through the Renault Design studios, including three of the current team directors at Peugeot Citroën.) But although the world of boats was new to me, I found myself working with a receptive and open-minded team: they, too, had not heard anything about 'Mickey Mouse ears' - apart from those they might have come across in a Disney theme park.

Thanks to my earlier professional experience I could see that VPLP was making a huge technological leap by adopting 3D design software, which is used in every automotive design centre and is ideally suited to the development of complex forms. New horizons have opened up since this software was brought in, and we swiftly became much more ambitious in our research into more complex shapes. We have also been able to find 'our' own magician, an ace at 3D, Frédéric Gasson, who has an automotive background and is still active in the sector. He has the benefit of extensive international experience and has worked for many brands, including Toyota, Renault and Bugatti. In addition to his instinctive appreciation of form, Frédéric has a great deal of technical knowledge and works on screen at a speed that my former colleague Mike Painter would never have believed possible.

Over the past few years I have been involved in the design of a great number of boats, all of them highly efficient and based on intelligent architectures; the great majority have been sailing catamarans. Just like seagulls, they flow with the wind, they show off and, all too often, they flaunt their beauty while at anchor. And in none of these boats is there the slightest sign of those 'Mickey Mouse ears', either to port or to starboard.

When parallels meet

It took artists and scientists hundreds of years to define the mathematical rules of perspective, which eventually were set during the Renaissance. However, long before that, architects had a thorough, if not completely theoretical, knowledge of these rules. So much so that they also knew that the human eye has its imperfections, and that bending the rules - and the lines - is sometimes necessary. Although Athens's Parthenon seems to be composed of perfectly straight lines, it is in fact full of slight curves, in order that we have a 'correct' view of it. Furthermore, its columns are slightly tilted inwards, so that if they rose to the sky, they would converge a mile above the temple. That tiny angle is invisible, and the lines of columns appear to be parallel, but the brain unconsciously translates it into an impression of strength. No wonder, then, that the famous Rolls-Royce grille was directly inspired by the Parthenon, and would also feature a slight convex curve to its face, so as to make it appear straighter and squarer. Well, this is the case on 'classic' Rolls-Royces; the recent Phantom, Ghost and Wraith now feature rather different versions of that grille, while retaining the same visual impact.

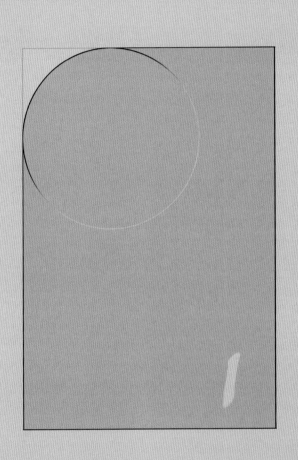 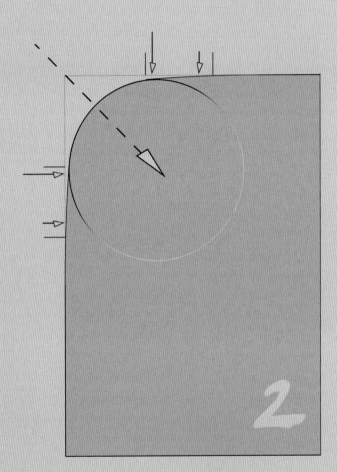

32

As Beautiful as a... Truck

Here's an act of irreverence on my part: I'm not going to talk about car design. Instead, I'll be talking about the design of trucks and other machines that go under the heading of commercial vehicles. I'll even go a step further and extend the discussion to coaches, buses and, yes, agricultural tractors. What all these vehicles have in common is that they are designed by designers – and that includes farm tractors. Just as tools can be beautiful (for example a pair of secateurs or an elegant hammer), so there can be farm tractors that are handsome or even superb.

But it was not always so. In the very early 1950s the majority of trucks were designed by whichever technician from the engineering department was the most proficient with a pencil. Only very rarely was the hand of an experienced professional stylist involved. Later, thanks to the influence from America, even trucks became fair game for the stylists and, from that point on, everything would begin to show a designer's touch. One of these trucks was the remarkable Stradair (1965), conceived for Berliet by the great designer Philippe Charbonneaux, who came up with a truck that was resolutely modern for its time. It had the frontal expression of a household appliance, and sported an extremely asymmetric grille – a characteristically French quirk that he later applied to the Renault 8 and 10 as well. Thanks to Charbonneaux the Stradair changed the way people viewed trucks in general, turning them into objects worthy of attention. And that, too, is when the French expression 'as beautiful as a truck' came to be coined.

When I started my career, in the late 1960s, there was still a noticeable hierarchy evident between those with the high status associated with designing the exterior of a car (even if the people with these privileges had not yet become divas) and the others – the poor unfortunates press-ganged into designing the interiors. Basically, the feeling was: interior styling equals inferior styling.

Of course there already were the 'not good enoughs' and those 'with one hand behind their back', who designed trucks and other industrial vehicles. Going further down the pecking order, there were those who seemed to be undergoing some kind of punishment, which took the form of designing interiors for trucks and buses. Then, a hundred metres below ground level: the tractor designers. And finally, below the floorboards, interior styling for tractors... a dungeon of despair, no less.

I was fortunate enough to take on a truck project at the time I got my first big promotion, as a studio director for Ford of Europe. This happened at the same time that the remarkable Bob Lutz, in the midst of his spectacular rise, advanced from executive vice-president of truck operations to president of Ford of Europe (see page 101). This was my first truck, and it was lucky for us that a car programme – the new Escort, the first of that model to switch to front-wheel drive – was absorbing all the attention of the senior design managers and of the organization in general. This provided us with a welcome undisturbed environment for our work and – although I hesitate to suggest there is any connection – the Cargo was voted European Truck of the Year following its release in 1981.

The Cargo's very smooth and aerodynamic styling was distinguished by an important innovation: a tall glazed panel set into the lower half of each door, dramatically improving sideways visibility towards nearby cyclists and pedestrians. The interior was decidedly modern, too, with a dashboard inspired by the hi-fi systems of a prominent Danish manufacturer. For the upholstery we developed a brand-new op-art-style fabric, black with red stripes; this got such a good reception that Ford decided to use it on the sporting version of the Escort, the XR3. We were pretty proud of that, even though no mention was made of it in the press documentation for the Escort's launch: just imagine the reaction to the revelation that the sporty bucket seats of the halo model were clad in fabric from a truck!

Left to right:
The Renault Radiance concept truck, the Renault Agriculture Atlès 936 tractor and the Ford Cargo truck.

Some years later, after I had been hired to lead Renault Design, I was in charge of a large operation devoted to the design of trucks and vans, as well as agricultural tractors. I remember the start of the Atlès programme, which had as its mission to be the largest tractor in the Renault Agriculture range. The stipulation from the marketing directors was that the design should be very virile, so, in response, the head of the design team presented an enormous phallus in the guise of the engine cover. And that is precisely how the fullsize model was shown to the executive committee. The verdict was unanimously in favour of this design. No one mentioned the patently masculine character of the machine; we had simply fulfilled the design specification to the letter. This tractor is still in production, although nowadays the models are fluorescent green as the brand was acquired by the German agricultural machinery manufacturer Haas Maschinenbau.

The most stunning truck project I worked on was the Radiance, a concept vehicle presented at the 2004 Hanover motor show. Under the direction of the brilliant Xavier Allard, who is now design director at Alstom, a team comprising Julien Drouard for the highly expressive exterior and Fabrice Pouille for the interior came up with a design that for me is still a textbook example of elegance and simplicity. To this day, the Radiance concept retains a remarkable relevance to contemporary conditions. At the moment, it might be just out of reach, but it wouldn't be impossible to achieve in the longer run. This could well be the perfect definition of any concept car, truck or farm tractor – never mind what the purists might say about such an unconventional combination.

Heavy metal thunder

Since their sole purpose is to carry as much load as possible, shouldn't trucks, or lorries, be the most utilitarian means of road transport? Not really: to start with, the first cars were, strictly speaking, trucks. Nicolas Joseph Cugnot's 1771 *fardier* (dray) was meant to carry cannons, and Amédée Bollée's 1873 L'Obéissante, with its twelve-passenger capacity, was a bus. In addition, the fact that truck drivers lived on the road, constantly fettling their machines, gave birth to a mystique akin to the one surrounding sailors. Like sailors, truckers were strong; they could handle heavy, dangerous vehicles; they had tattoos; they met in roadside cafés in which a car driver would immediately feel ill at ease. And they could be scary, as Steven Spielberg brilliantly demonstrated in his 1971 film, *Duel*. Trucks themselves, be they American, British, French or from anywhere else, have often been designed to convey that feeling of absolute power. Some of them, like the British Foden F1 (1931), the American White (1932) designed by Victor Schreckengost, and the French Berliet Stradair (1965) penned by Philippe Charbonneaux, have become design icons in their own right. And the way truck drivers tend to customize their steers proves, once more, that trucks are definitely not simple tools.

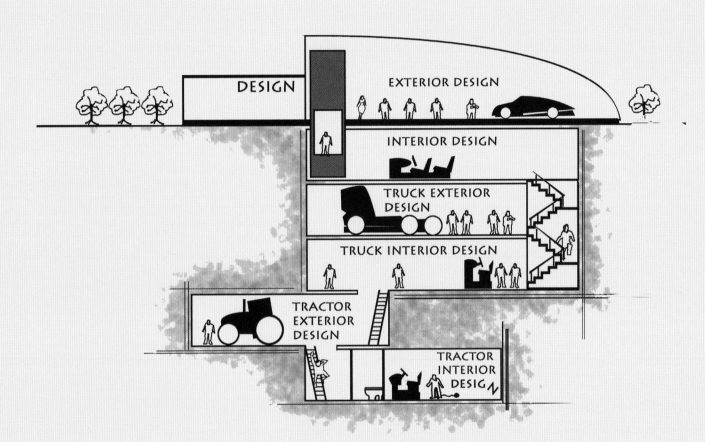

33

Logan: The Story of a Phenomenon

I t is rare that one can credit a brilliant idea to a single individual, especially when that idea proved to be as resounding a success as the Logan. But in this particular instance there's no debate whatsoever: the Logan and the low-cost revolution it inspired have just one father, and his name is Louis Schweitzer.

The idea came to the Renault president in the early 1990s during a trip to Russia with Manuel Gomez, who at the time was responsible for the company's international activities. While Louis Schweitzer was being driven through the streets of Moscow, his interest was sparked by the huge numbers of Lada Novas (Rivas in the UK) in circulation. The Nova was a small sedan derived from the 1960s Fiat 124 and was manufactured in Togliatti, a huge plant set up with the assistance of Fiat. The Nova project was sold to the Russians in exchange for the supply of sheet metal, one of whose properties was to rust, instantly. But, for the record, the 124 itself was known for its simplicity, its practicality and its ease of repair – which was just as well, for it was fond of breaking down.

During the course of the journey Schweitzer bombarded Gomez with questions about the omnipresent Nova and asked to be supplied with technical and commercial data on it. His intuition told him that there must also be enormous potential for a car like the Nova in the markets of eastern Europe as well as in every other developing country. And this, drawing its inspiration from the idea of a Lada-type product, led to the proposal to examine the concept of an affordable and cheap-to-run vehicle that was simple but both reliable and rugged in construction, and offered decent safety.

Today, in the knowledge of the spectacular breakthrough made by this model and its successors, you might think it would have been a simple matter for Schweitzer to set the programme in motion: after having had this great idea, there would be nothing left to do except complete the requisite paperwork. But when he came to share his idea with the executive committee the response was lukewarm, amounting to a complete rejection. For my part, just like Manuel Gomez, I was absolutely convinced and fired up by the company president's idea – with hindsight it seems so obvious – but I also have to say that for a long time we were the only two to support it. This comes through clearly in Schweitzer's comments on the genesis of the Logan, recorded by the Romanian journalist Dan Vardie in his 2010 book *Renault si Dacia. De 10 Ani Impreuna* (Renault and Dacia – 10 years together). In the book, Schweitzer acknowledges our support for the project, as well as its almost unanimous rejection by everyone else in the company; more particularly, he remembers that the engineers regarded this project for a so-called €5000 car as a retrograde move that went against the tide of history.

Before the Logan project was opened up to the designers, as Renault Design did for every new programme, we issued an internal invitation to anyone who wanted to take part in this first round of the creative process. But, given the very specific nature of the brief, we had no idea what to expect: would the team be ten? Fifteen? Or a lot fewer? Stepping into the meeting room, I received a great and positive surprise. Not only were all the seats already occupied, but many more designers were cramming the room, standing in the aisles or seated on the floor. We had never before attracted so many designers to a project. As the American designer Charles Eames suggested, constraints are the designer's best friend, and to my astonishment all these designers relished the opportunity to take up a challenge that some in the company believed to be impossible.

The excitement became so contagious that it spread to all who had been selected in the other departments involved. A good number of them, however, did feel their nomination to be a form of demotion. But that proved to be short-lived as Gérard Detourbet, the programme director, was able to instil a pioneering spirit of frugal innovation, which helped to draw in those who were the most sceptical. Everyone wanted to contribute to the optimization of

Louis Schweitzer eyeing the Lada Nova/Riva.

costs: reducing the number of stamping operations, cutting down material wastage, identifying components that could be carried over from existing vehicles, and minimizing the investment necessary. Optimization could also take the form of making a component perform multiple functions, as well as simplifying the assembly tasks.

All this resulted in a vehicle that was very practical and effective, even if it was no ravishing beauty – despite the clear talent of Benoit Jacob who, incidentally, also designed the fabulous Renault Sport Spider (see page 148). One of the reasons for this lack of glamour was that the Logan had been given very upright bodysides (usually more the preserve of a commercial vehicle rather than a three-box sedan) so that the doors could be shared with the station wagon version, which was to be especially roomy so as to provide space for three adults in the third row of seats.

In spite of its lack of conventional charm, the Logan met the programme's highly ambitious cost targets perfectly, and towards the end of its development we were even offered a few euros more to upgrade the model further. Sadly, the offer came too late. The Logan proved to be much more than simply an instant success in its launch markets of eastern Europe in 2004: very rapidly, strong pressure built up for the model to be introduced into the rest of Europe, too. In the case of the latter, it appealed to a customer base, overlooked until that point, seeking a no-frills vehicle that would provide mobility on a tight budget; it also appealed to other groups of customers, often comfortably off, who wanted to step off the bandwagon of always frantically adding more and more content into vehicles. In western Europe, too, the Logan and its derivatives turned into a huge commercial success story. Within a few years, after having rolled out a policy of even broader market coverage under a variety of badges (Dacia, Renault or Nissan, depending on the territory), the Dacia range became globally the most profitable of the whole Group.

So, to summarize, the Logan introduced a new blueprint for project management as well as a new approach enabling engineers, designers and marketing people to work together much more effectively. And in so doing, it provided confirmation that when it comes to sparking innovation, it is better for people to synchronize their brainpower than to bash their heads together.

Working-class heroes

The idea of creating a car that most people can afford is almost as old as the automobile itself, and the Model T Ford was arguably the first of them. Still, things were easier in 1908, since almost no other choice was available: although the Ford had been designed for a rural country with very poor roads, as the USA was then, it was at the time also good enough for countries where the road network was much more efficient, such as Britain or France. The Model T's affordability was relative: in today's money, its 1908 price of $850 translates to about $21,000 (£16,000). Likewise, the VW Beetle's shortcomings could be forgiven only in an impoverished post-war Europe at first, then in much poorer countries. What the car can do matters as much as price: the minimal Voisin Biscooter was a cramped, slow contraption with only two seats; more recently, the Tata Nano was a resounding failure. Although very affordable, it was too small and too slow, too. Worse, it had 'poverty' written all over it, so much so that Indians preferred buying bigger second-hand cars that were less revelatory of their social status. A car for the working classes needs to be classless, like blue jeans.

34

Concours d'Élégance

The first time I took part in an automobile *concours d'élégance* was in 1988. That was the year I was invited to join the jury for the Louis Vuitton Classic at the Parc de Bagatelle, part of the Bois de Boulogne in Paris. The president of the jury at the time was a legend in the world of collectors' cars, Christian Philippsen, who could always be spotted in a crowd thanks to his distinctive bright red trousers – a sartorial detail that was then rather unique and which testified to his strong character. But more than anything, the scarlet shade bore witness to his everlasting passion for the red rocketships produced by the Commendatore Ferrari: after all, Christian had been president of the French Ferrari Club for many years.

I never missed a single *concours* organized by Christian. Each one was just as intoxicating as the one before, and I never grew tired of the exceptional cars on display. Even after having had the pleasure of spending three or four days surrounded by these automotive masterpieces I found that my capacity for amazement had remained undiminished – in contrast to some people who have the task of dealing with these cars on a day-to-day basis. They run the risk of getting used to everything, even the best, and a sort of numbing takes over: they may not look any more, and the extraordinary can become routine and ordinary. Absence makes the heart grow fonder, so it is said, and this, en passant, strengthens a conviction I always had about Henry Ford II, grandson of the company founder, and the head of the organization where I worked for so long. An obsessive devotee of Château Margaux, that magnificent red Bordeaux that can be kept for a century and which has an astonishing length in the mouth, Mr Ford could not have continued to flatter his palate with this exceptional wine because by drinking it at every meal I imagine he must have ended up no longer appreciating its true taste. The moral of the tale is that you get used to everything, even to the very best wine.

All this led me to conclude that it was unwise to 'binge' on beauty, for fear of losing my own sense of wonderment. So, from then on, my wife and I adopted a policy of having two different homes, the first being in the Paris area and the second in Cassis on the south coast of France, just where the famous *calanques* (sheltered inlets) begin. By switching between these every three weeks we have been able to avoid suffering from our senses being swamped, and never lose touch with the appreciation of the truly exceptional – in this case the vista on show every evening as the sun sets over the Mediterranean and Cap Canaille.

But back to our four-wheeled masterpieces. It is currently held that collectors' cars represent the best of all possible investments, better than bricks and mortar, the stock market or gold. And it is all too true that the value of certain automobiles has shot up to such stratospheric heights that, because of the fear of accident damage, they have become 'auto*immobiles*' stuck in their secure air-conditioned garages. After all, who in their right mind would risk losing everything purely for the trifling pleasure of a quick trip around the block? The answer is clear: no one. Most of the time, outings for these types of cars are limited to being airfreighted in containers, accompanied by a retinue of servants skilled in the use of the feather duster on coachwork or tweezers for extracting blades of grass that have so unhelpfully lodged themselves between the tread blocks of the tyres. And then there are also the racing cars whose entire bodywork has been panel-beaten into perfect shape by genius sheet-metal masters – who have nothing in common with the people who originally hammered them out on the edge of a workbench. Back in the day, these gleaming monsters, with small surface imperfections that bore witness to the speed with which they were built, were designed not for parading around in sanitized surroundings but for battling their way to the top step of the winner's podium.

Christian Philippsen.

Even though I have never been an avid student of the history of the automobile, I have been fortunate enough to meet other members of the jury who know that history perfectly, not just as observers but also as those who were part of the action. The personalities have all been remarkable, too. Paul Frère, for instance – a true gentleman from Belgium who, after a sparkling career as a racing driver (his victories include the 24 Hours of Le Mans in 1960), became a great motoring journalist. I could also mention Sergio Pininfarina, son of Battista Farina who was known as Pinin (Turin dialect for 'small'); on the death of his father, Sergio took up the reins of the company to write still more chapters in the history of the family organization behind the design of the most beautiful Ferraris. Also Hervé Poulain, the celebrated auctioneer and racing driver emeritus, and Serge Bellu, the well-known journalist and former editor-in-chief of the magazine *Automobiles Classiques* as well as the author of one of my biographies. And I should not forget Gordon Murray, the outstanding South African-born engineer who conceived no fewer than twenty-two Formula One cars for the Brabham and McLaren teams;

for the record, he was also the engineer behind the original McLaren F1 road car; its exterior design was done by one of my former students at the Royal College of Art in London, Peter Stevens. In the early 1990s this was the ultimate supercar, with its distinctive three-seater layout and a 627 horsepower V12 engine directly behind those bucket seats.

And to tell the truth it was through contact with people like these that I too began to yearn to share a part of my life with a Ferrari. It proved a heady experience, and one that lasted six years. It was the purchase of a 328 GTB, a car that had always touched my heart and even my soul, that enabled me to discover a whole new dimension of automobile emotion: mechanical beauty. I came to understand the exceptional precision with which the pinions in a Ferrari gearbox were machined, and how the driver needs to start off in second gear until the gearbox oil temperature has risen sufficiently to allow first to be used. And then there is always speed! As the French novelist Françoise Sagan put it so aptly, 'If you've never loved speed, you've never loved life.' But that's another story…

Portrait of the artist as a car lover

Automotive design is an art in its own right. This is probably the reason why many artists have been genuinely keen on cars, either personally or as a source of inspiration, or both. The BMW 'Art Cars' that started in 1975 with a BMW 3.0 CSL painted by Alexander Calder were not the first cars to inspire artists: the Ukrainian-born French cubist artist Sonia Delaunay decorated a Bugatti Type 35 in 1924, a Citroën 5CV in 1925 and a Matra M530 in 1967. On the musical side, the Austrian conductor Herbert von Karajan and the American trumpeter Miles Davis, although radically different, shared a passion for fast cars, including a huge number of Porsches for the former and a Lamborghini Miura for the latter, while former Pink Floyd drummer Nick Mason is now as well known for his car collection as for his music. In the world of literature, Arthur Conan Doyle was one of the first motorists in Britain. But movies are the medium with the closest links with cars. After all, they were born together and, as George Lucas (whose *American Graffiti* of 1973 is a hymn to the American automobile culture) once put it, 'Cinema is the only art that can capture that adrenaline rush of racing speeds.'

35

French Racing Blue

I returned to France for good in 1987, after having spent almost thirty years of my life abroad. Following my years at school and university in England, as a young graduate I had married my sweetheart and started my career in the French automotive industry when, together with my business partner, John Pinko, we founded the Style International design agency (see page 29). But not long afterwards, after we had lost all our contracts in the wake of the upheavals of May 1968, I left my beautiful country – only to return nineteen years later as director of design for Renault.

After such a long time abroad, living in turn in Great Britain, in Germany and finally in the United States, I felt the need to find my bearings in France once again, especially when it came to dealing with the great French administrative machine. I remember reading a letter from one of these services and finding myself completely taken aback by how hard it was to understand what the letter was about. For sure, I was able to understand each word in isolation, but it was almost impossible to grasp the actual meaning of the whole.

Of course we French are complicated beings, and of course we are perplexing. By way of evidence, just look at our numbering system. How could we have accepted the seventeenth-century findings of the expert grammarian and Académie Française member Claude Favre de Vaugelas, as well as the authors of the Academy's dictionary, and adopted the forms 'sixty-ten' (*soixante-dix*), 'four-twenty' (*quatre-vingt*) and 'four-twenty-ten' (*quatre-vingt-dix*) instead of the seventy (*septante*), eighty (*octante*) and ninety (*nonante*) used by our Swiss and Belgian friends? In France I have often noticed that when faced with a problem that needs to be solved, our authorities tend to set up a commission that invariably leads to the identification of many more problems. Yet none of this has ever prevented me from being struck both by the high level of general culture of the people it is my pleasure to mix with, and by the very visible demonstrations of French genius. This is amply illustrated by the many remarkable achievements of our engineers, our architects and also our designers. France is well known as the country of lightness, though in this instance I'm not referring to our spirits or our moral values but rather to the ceaseless striving for lightness in our engineering – even though this much-lauded ethos of 'always less' contrasts starkly with the 'more and more' espoused by our governments.

Lightness is ever present in our genes as the inspiring spirit that urges us to seek the lightest possible solution. My designer's intuition immediately associates this with intelligence at its purest level, whether that's in the work of civil engineer Gustave Eiffel (such as Paris's Eiffel Tower, 1889), of aviation pioneer Gabriel Voisin or of Jean Rédélé with his 1950s–1970s Alpine sports cars. Further proof that lightness is hard-wired into our DNA comes from the celebrated British engineer Isambard Kingdom Brunel: was he not of Huguenot descent? His creations revolutionized public transport and engineering in nineteenth-century Britain, and he was the author of numerous innovations in the construction of bridges, tunnels, ships and railways, most especially the elegant and lightweight structures of the Great Western Railway and the famous London to Bristol line.

The history of the French automobile industry is full of celebrated examples in which lightness has been used to great effect. That had already become true before World War I after aircraft engineers had shown how to build structures that were both light and strong, putting an end to the old adage that only heavyweight construction could do the job. This was reaffirmed after World War II when the pursuit of lightness became a priority in the struggle to reduce fuel consumption, something that prompted the great automobile engineer Jean-Albert Grégoire to remark that 'lightness has proved itself the most noble element in engineering excellence.'

The outcome of all this was a magnificent series of lightweight coupés, the most beautiful and most successful of which was

The Renault Sport Spider.

the fabulous Alpine A110 (1961), shaped by Giovanni Michelotti, the man said to have been behind more than one thousand designs. When I arrived at Renault one of my dreams was to revive the legend of the Alpine A110 – even though at that exact same time, and with me being a powerless onlooker, I witnessed the market launch of the A610 (1991). This was that dreadful Alpine designed for the US market and conceived by people who, without realizing it, were trampling all over the DNA of the marque, of which only the heritage and the name survived. But what a name!

Soon after I took up my role at Renault I launched a programme of special projects allowing each designer to come up with their individual ideas, with the design directors overseeing the overall management, and this practice has continued over the years. Over the course of the years that followed, this enabled us to present a series of Alpine proposals. A one-fifth scale model of one of these enjoyed pride of place in Carlos Ghosn's office from his arrival in the company as executive vice-president in 1996 until the day he left for Japan some three years later to revive Nissan. Many were the occasions on which we tried to get our top management interested, but each time we came up against the stumbling blocks of the business case and a general lack of enthusiasm. Fortunately, this did not prevent us producing a very small run of an 'image' model that went under the name of Spider and which was heavily influenced by Renault Design's first concept car, first shown in 1990, the Laguna roadster. Designed by the very gifted Benoit Jacob, the Spider was conceived as an Alpine but when the project was announced internally there was such an outcry and such opposition from the marketing department that, together with Christian Contzen, my friend and ally at Renault Sport, we decided not to run the risk of losing everything. And so, during the time it took to develop the vehicle, we set aside our campaign to promote the revival of the Alpine brand, knowing that in return we would be allowed to pursue the Spider programme under the Renault Sport label. But in order to respond to the concerns of the company's president, Louis Schweitzer, regarding the crashworthiness of this very sporty car, we were obliged, much to our regret, to add a lot of weight to the all-aluminium chassis.

And that was how we then came to find ourselves at some considerable remove from the original Alpine ethos; 'too heavy, my son', is what Jean Rédélé might have said.

Light programme

'Light is right': although the art of designing light cars seems to be a French speciality, this sentence was the motto of a quintessentially British car maker, Colin Chapman. Chapman shared his obsession with lightness (which actually sometimes went too far, where his racing cars were concerned) with René Bonnet of DB, Jean Rédélé of Alpine and André Lefèbvre, father of the 2CV (see page 165), and for the same reason: namely, the inability to source powerful engines. Had Chapman been able to source a more powerful engine than an Austin 7's to propel his Lotus Mark I in 1948, things might have been different. Other British manufacturers of the time, such as Allard or Jensen, chose a radically different way. In France, no real alternative was available: the tax system favoured small, often good engines, and until 1973 it was impossible to buy a French car with more than four cylinders, apart from a handful of Talbots and Bugattis immediately post-war, and the ill-fated (and Chrysler-powered) Facel Végas of the 1960s. Whether in Britain or in France, the situation made for great cars, and still does: driving a Lotus Elise is amazingly rewarding, and Renault has put remarkable efforts into limiting the weight of the new Alpine A110, with similar benefits.

36

Let's Play Catch-up

In the French motor industry we call it Phase II, but the English translate it as 'facelift'. This description has the virtue of being more visual than the French version because it makes the connection with cosmetic surgery, which offers a very close parallel with the physical process the car is subjected to. As a designer I really like the idea of a 'catch-up session' – an apt and equally graphic description of the approach taken by marketing directors when, three or four years after a car's launch, they decide to give it a light (or comprehensive, depending on the situation) refresh to secure the now-ageing model a second lease of life in the market. This is a sure way to revive the fortunes of a model, firstly by correcting any deficiencies reported by existing customers and also by bringing it up to date with competitors' vehicles that have been launched onto the market more recently.

Very often the teams responsible for the original design are brought back together to organize the relaunch operation, and each of the people involved has his or her own story and individual frustrations and disappointments. But my experience in the design profession has taught me that rather than refighting old battles, it is better to look straight ahead to the future, without so much as a sideways glance.

The starting point for a facelift programme is always the first set of feedback from the markets, and this information is generally accompanied by an analysis of the competition and various financial scenarios. These first impressions should be treated with caution; often, they can be misleading as it is too early to have sufficient perspective, though for Renault a persistent issue over several years was the criticism that its cars had a lower level of 'perceived quality' than those of the German brands. It should be remembered that although the top priority in the development of a new model is to please the customer, there is another important thread running through the process: to make sure the model

is profitable. Even so, this did not prevent certain programme directors from displaying the annoying tendency of never providing sufficient budget to get models launched with enough in the way of decorative highlights. The puzzling thing here was that this would never happen with commercial vehicles, nor for that matter with the models in the budget Dacia range. So, paradoxically, a Logan (see page 140) would sport more chrome detailing than a Clio. Try to figure that one out…. Yet when it came to facelift time the models being updated would – at last! – be treated to the proper allocation of decoration that had been specified originally, but which had been refused by the Mr Scrooge of the time.

In the 1980s automakers had smaller model ranges than they do these days, so the models had to have longer lifespans. The facelift had a much greater importance then, for products could begin to appear dated midway through their lives, and the profitability of the organization needed to be assured. Besides, in those days car makers were willing to allocate much bigger budgets to facelifts than they are today: the refresh could even go as far as updating all the body panels, with only the doors and the windscreen frame carried over.

This was certainly the case for two projects in which I was personally involved as the designer, the Ford Taunus/Cortina II and the Granada II. These were what were termed 'reskin' operations and, to pursue the cosmetic surgery parallel still further, they did indeed involve a new outer skin. It should be pointed out that when it came to launching reskinned designs the company was perfectly happy to describe them as new models, even though the interior, the dashboard and the door panels were unchanged apart from some fresh colours and trim materials.

It was the same at Volkswagen, where I was put in charge of the facelift for the Golf II in 1989. We updated the front end by introducing fully enveloping plastic bumpers, an innovation the Renault 5 had pioneered in 1972. At the rear, however, we could not change the original sheet-metal work as there had been no provision for fitting this type of bumper, so in order to achieve a balanced appearance between front and rear we had to cheat and apply a dummy bumper moulding.

Sometimes facelifted models are overloaded with add-ons that give the impression of being afterthoughts – much as on a Venetian carnival mask – rather than improvements. But in the majority of instances these operations work as planned and enhance the image of the model to give a genuine boost to its sales figures. The Renault 19 is a case in point. In its original form it was somewhat austere, but the designers' touches on the facelifted version made it much more attractive and turned it into a huge sales success. But my favourite 'Phase II' is still the Twingo. Over the course of the years it traded in its grey-on-grey bumpers in favour of a new set finished in body colour, and its famous half-moon gaze was enhanced by a bit of 'eye make-up' in the form of a more sophisticated treatment for the headlights' interior components.

But sometimes a wrong detail can wreck everything, as with the Clio II. When it was launched in 1998 it was one of the few remaining cars in the market to feature glass lenses, with their dated ribbed design, for its headlamps instead of polycarbonate material. It should be noted that in this case we were dealing with a programme director who had little awareness of the trends of the time, and still less sense of the broader sweep of design evolution; the latter would completely transform the frontal signature of cars thanks to the move from glass headlight lenses to clear polycarbonate material. When I bumped into Giorgetto Giugiaro at the Geneva motor show the year the Clio II was launched, he said with a little wink: 'I like the car a lot, but it's a shame about the headlights.' This small detail, which in actual fact was much more than a detail, was corrected when it came to the Phase II facelift, earning me a belated but unexpected compliment from a passer-by I overheard in the trendy Canal Saint-Martin district in Paris: 'You've got beautiful eyes, you know.'

They shoot horses, don't they?

As with the ones performed on human beings, automobile facelifts aim to bring back youth to an ageing product, as if it were a man or a woman past his or her prime. And as with aesthetic surgery, the results can vary from the great (Flaminio Bertoni's fairing of the DS front lights in 1967) to the ridiculous, or even the pathetic. Interestingly, the result is not always proportional to the amount of work involved: Citroën's pug-ugly Visa of 1978 suddenly became much more palatable when, in 1982, it was given a new grille, new wheels and a dash of black paint under the rear window, which made it seem much larger. No new pressings, limited investments, better sales: job done. However, although not particularly beautiful, the Visa had an asset: it was young, and as such could suddenly seem lovely, Cinderella-like, with just a slight touch of 'make-up'. Still, be it with cars or with people, no amount of work will ever be able to hide old age. Even Italdesign's talent could not do anything to save from infamy the 1980 Morris Ital, in effect a tarted-up 1971 Marina, which itself used parts that sometimes had been designed decades before.

37

If I Had a Hammer

Trini Lopez, the American singer of Mexican extraction, released his single 'If I Had a Hammer' in 1963 – and when I happened to hear it recently, it suddenly made me wonder. How would I, if I could turn back the clock and with the aid of my own hammer, set about modifying the many automotive creations I have contributed to over the years? Some of these products, dating from the early days of my career at Ford in Britain, are not worthy of mention as I was playing only a small part at a time when marketing and product planning were frequently controlled by Americans who had been sent to Europe to build their careers. Or they could have been sent here to get them out of the way of head office in Detroit; or dispatched as penance for an earlier crime, as was the case with the notorious Roy Brown, father of the Edsel, who found himself exiled to Europe for several years in the wake of the sales fiasco surrounding that model.

After I had moved to Germany, I designed several cars, such as the 1976 Taunus/Cortina, which from a design point of view were pretty well on the right track – even though when confronted with the reality of a twisty mountain road it was a somewhat different story. Then there were the Capris, successive generations of the Fiesta and, finally, the Sierra. This last had us quaking with fear throughout its gestation, for we were taking a big gamble in embarking on a whole new stylistic direction in a mid-market car. And it is worth pointing out that it was at the same Paris motor show that Citroën launched its BX, a design that was as stiff as a board. What happened next was sadly rather less glorious: although the Sierra was a big sales success, the larger Scorpio, built on the same platform but with tiny 14-inch wheels in its entry-level form, was a flop; in truth, it did look uncomfortably like an old-style roller skate.

In 1987 I joined Renault and stayed for twenty-two years. I was lucky enough to lead a highly talented team, a team that had for a long time been forced to submit to the diktat

of the engineering fraternity. Together, we succeeded in developing genuinely good cars, some of them with strong personalities.

I won't hark back to the Twingo (see page 76) as, to cite Antoine de Saint-Exupéry's pronouncement on perfection (see page 130), there is no need to add anything, nor take anything away. But I do regret the front-end design of the first-generation Scénic: it was horribly fussy, although this didn't prevent the model being a runaway success and breaking all sales records, with as many as 1800 buyers a day. I am also still gratified whenever I see a second-generation Mégane hatchback on the road, its style directly drawn from the Vel Satis concept car (not to be confused with the series-production model bearing the same name, a design that deserves two or three blows of my hammer on account of its ungainly proportions).

And while I am about it I would give a few very gentle hammer taps to the Avantime (see page 120) to give it a bit more softness, because at the time its designer had the unfortunate weakness of failing to distinguish between tension and stiffness. Incidentally, after that same designer had left the Espace IV project to take up a promotion, we had to completely reassess all the volumes of the design proposal in order to give it more gentleness or, as former Citroën and subsequently Style Renault director Robert Opron would have said, more mellowness.

I really liked the third-generation Mégane: its objective was to help evolve Renault design towards more muscular forms. I particularly liked the coupé version, which my very talented successor as design director, Laurens van den Acker (see page 182), enhanced quite brilliantly through a facelift of the front end. Yet this derivative very nearly failed to see the light of day: when the styling proposals were presented to Renault's top management, the product planning director described it as not a proper Renault, dismissing it as exceptionally aggressive. Mercifully, he was the only one to express that opinion and the rest of the

The Citroën BX (far left) and the Ford Sierra.

committee gave it a much more enthusiastic welcome. For the unfortunate individual this meant the end of an era, and the Mégane III proved to be his swansong.

And then there are all those cars from rival French brands that I have either loved or loathed. Take the Citroën Ami 6, for example: here, I must confess that even though I am not a violent person, I would be tempted to deal it several well-aimed sledgehammer blows. Not in order to improve it by reshaping its profile – an impossible aspiration in any case – but to punish it for having offended my eyes for so many years and for having presented such an atrocious image of French design to the rest of the world. How could the great Flaminio Bertoni have created the DS and then gone on to devise this monstrosity? In France meat eaters often say *'tout est bon dans le cochon'* (everything is good in the pig), but that was patently not the case with this particular pig of a car – if indeed you can flatter it with such a description.

On the other hand I would again congratulate Gérard Welter for his sublime Peugeot 205 GTI (see page 62) – but also direct quite a few hammer blows at the Citroën Saxo and Peugeot 106, models highly regarded by no one except analysts devoid of any passion for cars. Strangely enough, these two utterly soulless designs were selected by Renault as the official benchmarks for the Twingo II programme and, in spite of the very best efforts of the design department, we could not get management to see our point of view. After the fabulous first-generation Twingo it was a huge let-down to see its name demoted to the ranks of cars with no soul.

One last observation, on the subject of concept cars: these are generally the area in which designers are allowed their greatest freedom of expression, and it is here that you can best judge the true creative prowess of a team and get a sense of the frustration involved in everyday tasks that are often so far removed from those dreams.

Relieving the tension

It is often said that the first concept car created as such was Harley Earl's 1938 Buick Y-Job. The assertion is debatable, since unique cars such as Edsel Ford and Bob Gregorie's 1932 Model 40 roadster could easily qualify as concepts, and so could one-offs from the beginnings of the automobile, such as Castagna's 1914 Alfa 40-60 HP. Whatever, concept cars often epitomize the design personality of a brand, freed from any regulations. They also are a useful relief for designers who constantly have to take into account the constraints of production and homologation in their daily work, not to mention the pressure of accountants and marketing people. A concept car has no prospective customers, will never be produced, and can break as many creative moulds as it wishes. It does not even need to work properly, although many do (the Y-Job was Earl's personal car for years). In the stressed universe of design studios, working on a concept car is akin to a play day during which everything is allowed, even imagining cars the company's management strictly forbids. This means that, although many concept cars often are proudly displayed in motor shows, some of them remain hidden in design studios, away from prying eyes - and, unfortunately, away from car lovers.

38

At Full Throttle

On a personal level, the car that did the most to initiate me into the world of out-and-out acceleration is the AC Cobra of the 1960s. The concoction fashioned by the US automotive designer and racing driver Carroll Shelby delivered acceleration that was astonishing for the time, reaching 60 mph in just over 4 seconds. The Cobra was based on the very British AC-Bristol, itself inspired by the very pretty Ferrari 166 MM Spider designed in 1948 by the head of Touring, Carlo Anderloni (see pages 193, 194). As was so perceptively observed by Bob Lutz, my boss at Ford for many years, 'when it comes to stealing, a bank is better than the local corner shop.'

The Cobra is the quintessential embodiment of the American motorsport spirit and its dream of one day beating Ferrari in the 24 Hours of Le Mans. Everyone knew that American cars of that era had about as much roadholding as a bar of soap in a bidet, but when it came to acceleration, they could *really* accelerate! When I was young I personally paid the price. It was my first time out in a 1968 Pontiac GTO, a powerful muscle car that Ford of Britain's competitor vehicle department had specially ordered with a three-speed manual transmission: they did this so that we Europeans would not be disorientated by this very non-European car which, like all American cars of the time, was originally designed around an automatic transmission. As fate would have it, however, my test drive one rainy evening was cut short as I braked too hard for a roundabout in Essex. My wife alongside me, we left the road and demolished a badly sited lamp post, cutting the car in half. We spent the night in hospital, but with a few stitches as the only consequence of the crash: mercifully, and ahead of its time, the GTO had been fitted with three-point seat belts.

Some years later, in the United States, I enjoyed some great times with a Mustang Shelby GT350, which was also adept at ripping up the tarmac. And it was in a Mustang, this time a third-generation model, that my wife and I took part in a driving skills course where we learned to master the art of the J-turn, an evasive manoeuvre in the security repertoire that helps to avoid the risk of kidnap. Fortunately for us, we have never had occasion to put this training into practice. Next, it was Germany and several years at the wheel of Ford Capris, including the famed RS. Although a lot lighter than their cousin and source of inspiration, the Mustang, the two had one feature in common: a live rear axle, which could require the driver to practise the art of opposite-lock cornering. This might have been fun for the driver, but that pleasure was definitely not shared by the passengers.

All this was in a bygone era when there was less traffic, speeds were still unlimited, and we used to drive at more than 140 mph in a V8-engined Audi on the *Autobahn* leading to the iron curtain dividing Germany's two halves – a route that just happened to be usefully free of traffic. Throughout my two years at Volkswagen in the mid-1980s I was a regular user of this section of *Autobahn*, linking Braunschweig and the VW Group headquarters at Wolfsburg, by the East German border, foot always flat to the floor.

And then the world changed. External pressures forced us to drive much more slowly because roads were becoming increasingly clogged up with traffic and enforcement of speed limits became ever stricter right across Europe, and also because of the realization that speed really does kill. All of us knew people who had become victims of the roads. Yet, in one of life's strangest paradoxes, the past few years have seen a multitude of supercar launches, among them Bugatti with its Veyron, and numerous Ferraris and Lamborghinis. But most of all, there has been Gordon Murray's fabulous McLaren F1 (see page 146): this goes straight to the top step of the podium. More recently, Aston Martin unveiled what the world had been breathlessly awaiting: the Valkyrie, conceived by Red Bull racing designer Adrian Newey and capable of accelerating to 60 mph in 2.5 seconds. I struggle to imagine what kind of person

The Pontiac GTO.

would be prepared to lay down three million dollars for the privilege of getting to 60 mph that quickly. Because, and do take note, this is not a track-only car: that one is still to come, and it will be even faster.

Will the happy owners of such a car spend their lives in a permanent whirlwind? Might we expect them to gulp their dinner down in 4.5 seconds, stopwatch in hand? Or to get dressed in less than two? And could the next supercar be faster still – so fast, in fact, that it will already have reached 60 mph even before its computer-controlled butterfly doors have had the chance to open?

Over the course of fifty-five years we have succeeded in compressing the time needed to reach 60 mph by 1.5 seconds. What progress! What a triumph for our civilization, and what an eloquent demonstration of the ingenuity of the human race...

For my own part, I'll now be ambling along peacefully in a Jeep Wrangler, and I must confess that I have no idea how long it would take me to reach 60 mph from a standing start. You will probably be surprised that I have never bothered to ask myself that question. But from now on, the most important things for me as I drive are what's going on on the roads and pavements around me, and my ability to marvel at the visual spectacle of the Provençal countryside unrolling in front of my eyes.

No limits

For years, the AC Cobra, especially in its 427 version, remained the fastest-accelerating production car in the world, going from 0 to 60 mph in just over 4 seconds, but its barn-like aerodynamics limited its top speed. Its coupé version, prepared for racing, addressed the problem so well that it famously reached 185 mph on a British motorway in 1964, causing a public uproar and supposedly prompting the introduction of an experimental 70 mph speed limit that remains to this day. But AC was not the only manufacturer to test its cars on public roads: browsing the internet, it is possible to watch on-board footage of Stirling Moss before a race at Le Mans, testing a D-Type Jaguar around the roads that make up most of the circuit, crossing bikes, overtaking tractors, dodging traffic, as was common until the 1970s. Well into the 1990s, the German racing driver-cum-banker Thomas Bscher almost daily topped 200 mph during his commute to his office in his McLaren F1, as testified by the engine control unit data downloaded by McLaren. And to this day, the police avoid being too present on some of the roads around Maranello (home to Ferrari and the Scuderia Ferrari Formula One racing team), Sant'Agata Bolognese (Lamborghini), Zuffenhausen (Porsche) and Ingolstadt (Audi).

39

The Cars in My Life

I began my driving career in the same way as everyone else, in a fabulous convertible. It was one of those beautiful English models, most likely a Wolseley – the marque that, so I always remind the car connoisseurs I meet, was Great Britain's biggest carmaker in the early 1920s. This particular micro-cabriolet was equipped with pedals and drew much of its inspiration from the Wolseley Messenger. I came across it when my mother, who was British by birth, brought my siblings and me to visit her parents just after World War II. My passion for cars was probably born at that precise moment, in London when I was three and a half years old, and that passion has never left me.

Being able to drive was a total fixation for me throughout my adolescence: I quite simply could not wait until I was eighteen, and I do have to admit it… I didn't wait. After the death of my father, who was a great car lover, my mother bought herself a Citroën 2CV, and it was in this magnificent André Lefèbvre invention that I learned to drive. André Lefèbvre, who studied engineering at the École Supérieure d'Aéronautique in Paris, began his career working for Gabriel Voisin, the designer of many remarkable aircraft and, later, cars. He left Voisin after one of its many bankruptcies, first moving to Renault and then, in 1933, to Citroën, where he spent the rest of his working life. As well as the 2CV (*la Deuche*, as it is affectionately called in France: a shortening of Deux Chevaux, or two horses, that 2CV stands for), Lefèbvre was responsible for the Traction Avant and no less a creation than the sublime DS – apropos of which Ferdinand Porsche declared: 'Never in my life have I seen so much innovation packed into an individual production car.'

Learning to drive in a 2CV is very different from learning in a conventional car, and it imprinted indelibly on my psyche that French genius was alive and well and that it was formed from a combination of intelligence and ingenuity. It is precisely this that is known in India as *jugaad*: the art of doing more with less, generally in difficult conditions such as those we were experiencing in France after the war. This particularly French quality is very real and is still flourishing, even if it seems to be slipping out of use in the world of cars. I have to own up to having driven without a licence, initially accompanied but later completely solo, although only on the narrow lanes in the Laragne-Sisteron region of Provence; at that time many of the villages there would see only three or four cars a day, each accompanied by frantic horn-tooting to scatter the local farmers' champion egg-laying hens from out of their path.

For me, getting my licence was as important a rite of passage as being awarded my diploma in industrial design. My first car, the one that kept me mobile throughout my time as a student in England at the Birmingham College of Art and Design, was a compact apple-green Commer Cob van, to which I had added red racing stripes to boost its maximum speed.

As soon as I returned to France I started looking for a second-hand car. It had to be a Simca, of course, as that was the company that gave me my first job and, besides, it allowed me to park in the firm's own car park. I was looking for a convertible to provide me with at least a fragment of the dream, despite the grey skies of Poissy, northwest of Paris. This led me to the purchase of a Simca Océane – a strange name for a convertible, especially as the coupé version was called Plein Ciel, or open sky. The Océane was a very pretty car, even if its profile resembled that of a banana, drooping at the front and also at the rear; designed by a team under Jean Daninos, head of coachbuilder Facel, it was built there too. Mine was finished in Blue Sky of Capri, complemented by a black leather interior to excellent effect. It was fitted with the Flash Spécial engine, a designation I imagined might have been dreamt up by a marketing veteran from Proctor & Gamble; nevertheless, this did not prevent it from reaching its top speed of 88 mph.

Not long afterwards, my wife and I began our tour of duty in England as newly-weds, having arrived with no more than a suitcase apiece and with a car budget that restricted us to a sensible first-generation Escort. A year later I received my first promotion and, along with it, the benefit in kind that was to change our lives: a company car. This meant that for the next forty years I never bought another car - except in 2002, the year I won the Lucky Strike Designer Award from the Raymond Loewy Foundation. The prize money was substantial, and this allowed me to buy a very beautiful Ferrari 328 GTB.

Throughout all those years I drove cars made by the companies I was working for: Fords, Volkswagens, Audis and Renaults. I went from an Escort Mexico to a series of Capri RSs and Sierra XR4s, with a detour in the USA in the shape of a Thunderbird and a Lincoln Mark III. Then came the era of the Audi 200s, one of which had a V8 engine, and finally, the Renaults. One of these, my first R25, was totally rethought, with a fresh interior and the dashboard wrapped in the same rust-coloured leather, and the exterior finished in a brand-new shade of pearlescent blue. Renault also provided me with convertibles, Clio RSs, and a Spider - and that's not forgetting all the competitor cars, from Mercedes to Ferrari, via the very endearing Lada Niva. In other words, mine was a life that revolved around steering wheels, bucket seats (when available) and the power of horses - a lot of horses, each one of them whinnying with delight.

Company cars, with a twist

One of the perks of belonging to the top management of a car company is being able to have special wishes satisfied, especially where company cars are concerned: bespoke colours and interiors, even specifications, amended to suit one's taste, sometimes extensively. If, surprisingly, Enzo Ferrari had rather mundane cars, including a Mini and a Peugeot 404, Ferry Porsche, son of Ferdinand, drove, among other rarities, a modest 914... equipped with the flat-8 engine from a racing 908, and a long-wheelbase, four-seater 928. Gianni Agnelli, the owner and president of Fiat, also treated himself to one-offs most of his life. But managing a design team can make things easier, as it means having access to panel-beaters, upholsterers, painters and all the rest. GM's Bill Mitchell almost never drove a standard production car, instead favouring concept cars, or at least cars and motorbikes that he had colour-coded to match his favourite suits. More discreetly, top executives have access to cars from many manufacturers, for evaluation purposes of course. And, more often than marketing men, engineers or accountants, designers tend to indulge in cars they love and admire, irrespective of their make: during the 1990s, one could often see Lamborghinis and Aston Martins in Peugeot's design centre car park.

The Cars in My Life

40

Those Last Three Centimetres

'If only we'd had three more centimetres to play with, everything would have been different.' How many times did I hear that heartfelt lament when a new car was given its first motor-show unveiling! It is the perennial complaint of a designer still frustrated at being denied the green light to increase the width of the vehicle; with those extra few centimetres the design would, without a shadow of a doubt, have been transformed into a true masterpiece, an icon of automotive design...

This process of cars being ever wider and ever longer becomes very clear if you look carefully at the relentless swelling in size of our vehicles across the span of several generations. Take the halo product of a major brand, the Volkswagen Golf. It is now moving into its eighth incarnation, the first one having come out in 1974; over the course of forty years its length has stretched by 55.5 cm and its width by 15 cm, while its height has shrunk by almost 3 cm. Even the VW Polo, in the segment below the Golf, is 35 cm longer than the first Golf. Yet by contrast the size of the spaces in underground car parks has remained fixed at 5 metres long and 2.5 metres wide – something that I imagine must make bodywork repair shops happy. This tendency for cars to expand has nothing to do with people becoming taller or larger; rather, it is down to the desire to achieve ever more seductive proportions and style. This phenomenon is evident across the board in the auto industry, whether in small cars, luxury sedans or even sports cars.

A case in point is the Ferrari 328 GTB I used to drive. When it came out in 1985 it was neat, agile, manoeuvrable and alert, and particularly well suited to the twisting mountain roads of the Alps. But now its descendant, the 488 GTB, has become an exhibitionist's car, the length having grown by 31 cm; worst of all, its width of 1.95 metres is a shocking 22 cm bulkier than that of the 328 GTB. So, aside from motorways, the 488 is much more at home on the boulevards of Los Angeles or even parked outside the casino in Macau. It's for this reason that I take my hat off to Renault for what it has achieved with the new Alpine A110, and I am sure that the programme director must have had to withstand a lot of pressure from many quarters to make the car bigger, even if only by three centimetres, just to make it more beautiful, more aggressive, lower and more ground-hugging, more trendy, and, and, and... the list goes on.

From the early 1980s, even though I was not able to be proactive in systematically developing solutions to reduce the size of our vehicles, I was a strong and early advocate for the miniaturization of individual components, thus freeing up more space inside our cars and, in turn, allowing our customers to choose smaller models that nevertheless gave them just as much room inside. At first glance, however, the results of this process seemed far from convincing. The space that had been freed up was quickly appropriated by safety equipment and a remarkable number of additional vehicle functions, each requiring that little bit of space. Regrettably, all these individual 'bits' add up to a lot – so when we get into certain models we feel like thanking their creators for at least having left 'a bit' of space for us people.

In an address that I had prepared for him for the 1985 Society of Automotive Engineers conference in Cologne, Ford Germany director Daniel Goeudevert said that in the future we would need to move towards greater miniaturization of components thanks to the advent of electronics, and also because the whole industry was in the process of reshaping itself. The industrial model for car manufacturers at the time was to have a multitude of individual components produced to order by a large number of smaller suppliers, and then for the automaker to fit these components on its main assembly line. One of the biggest problems was that the automakers themselves had to do the designing and engineering of all of these components, even though they had precious few specialists on hand. And because those experts were so thin on the ground they

A generic supercar and the compact electric Renault Twizy.

gradually lost touch with the major trends under way in the industry, turning them effectively into ex-experts.

Clearly, the future would belong to the major systems integrators such as Bosch, Valeo or Plastic Omnium. They possessed large engineering resources capable of taking on all aspects of the engineering development of, say, a dashboard and centre console module, over and above the basic design produced internally by the automaker's design department. Then, the integrators would take care of the manufacture of the modules and their timed delivery direct to the assembly line, ready to be fitted, in a process perfected by the Japanese and known as 'just in time'. At the time we were confident that these new initiatives would allow us to rethink the old practices, under which the manufacturer of a component felt entitled to reserve a space on the vehicle for that part, just as it had been doing for the past twenty years with no questions being asked. We were locked into a system that was frozen solid.

It is interesting to note that Elon Musk, co-founder and CEO of Tesla, a company that is entirely rooted in the twenty-first century, did more than just bank on fully electric vehicles: more significantly, he completely rethought how these cars were designed and assembled. As if by chance, this translated into a miniaturization of components, which in turn resulted in quite remarkable interior roominess. He is such a strong force, this Musk; perhaps he will now turn his magic powers to increasing the size of parking spaces....

Where have all the inches gone?

The 1965 Renault 16, admittedly a very clever example of packaging, could comfortably take five people and their luggage within its 4.25 metres. With the same length, the 1984 Renault Espace could even seat seven people. That is the length of today's Volkswagen Golf: a very good car indeed, but by no means adapted to a large family. Where has all that interior space gone? In creature comforts such as air conditioning, certainly, and in safety features such as side bars and airbags; all of which is positive. Still, one can't help thinking that in order to integrate all these elements, interior space was deliberately overlooked, probably for cost reasons (a miniaturized item like the McLaren F1 CD player is much more expensive than an off-the-shelf one), and maybe for pricing reasons, too: one can charge a premium for air conditioning, but not for interior space - unless of course the customer chooses a larger, and more expensive, model. So far, no specialists of conspiracy theories have worked on the fact that many modern cars seem to be designed to be cramped inside, equipment notwithstanding: how about transmission tunnels on the floor of front-wheel drive cars? Unavoidable necessity, or...?

Those Last Three Centimetres

41

My Years in the Shadows

I have never done time in prison, but I did spend more than four years in the shadows: in offices, in factories, in workshops, at dealerships, in design studios, and also in airports and on planes. All this without a break, just a few hours of downtime at the weekend, and without any holiday outside the August break. This was almost certainly the most intense period of my career, and it started in January 1995 when I was appointed to the CDR, Renault's board of directors. As well as becoming a member of the CDR I was also appointed senior vice-president of Quality for the Group, which involved responsibility for nearly 6000 employees – in addition to the 450 or so I already had under my charge in Design.

This appointment came as a surprise to many in the company, although not to me as I had accepted the job four months earlier, on condition that the news be kept under wraps during the intervening period. I was to replace a great authority, Pierre Jocou, high priest of Total Quality and a man highly regarded throughout the company as well as feared by many on account of his reputation for refusing to compromise on quality issues whenever these could affect the customer. He was immensely considerate towards me as he handed over his responsibilities: we knew each other well. He had been the main force behind a cross-divisional project I had led during the time when Raymond Lévy was president: designed to speed up the vehicle development cycle and time to production, the programme yielded excellent results, reducing the time to market by a third.

Pierre Jocou had been described as the most powerful man in Renault, for he had the authority to delay the launch of a vehicle if, in his judgement, that model did not show a big enough step up in quality. In one of our advertising campaigns he had been pictured, his back to the camera, above the strapline 'The sales director may be getting impatient, but if this man says no, it means no!' Jocou was a real colossus, and he later moved to the United States to take up the presidency

of Mack Trucks, part of the Renault Group.

Taking on my new role was the moment when my diary began to be controlled by the hands of the clock. I had two offices: one, just a few metres away from that of the company president, at Renault headquarters in Boulogne-Billancourt in the western suburbs of Paris; the other in the Technocentre, our design and development centre in Guyancourt, further out of the city. I spent most of my time dealing with quality-related issues, attending the full complement of the company's regular meetings and also those arranged by my secretary. This locked me into a succession of meetings, each lasting half an hour, and working days that began at 7 am and stretched beyond 7 pm.

What proved hardest at the beginning were the weekly Monday-morning CDR meetings, at which president Louis Schweitzer and the newly recruited technical director Carlos Ghosn were present, and at which I was to report back on urgent issues in the area of quality. Once a month I gave an hour-long presentation to the CDR looking at a particular issue in depth. To top it all, only a matter of months after my nomination the company embarked on a massive cost-saving initiative, something that left me fighting a lone battle in the CDR to defend our drive for quality – in the face of opposition from certain managers who were prepared to make compromises so as to extricate the company from the alarming financial situation it found itself in. The majority of Executive Committee members understood the necessity of short-term cutbacks to save the company, while those of us responsible for Quality, well aware of the expectations of our customers, wanted to continue to improve our reputation in this area. There were some very difficult moments, and all too often I had to raise my voice or put my foot down. Sometimes decisions went against me, but I persisted. We succeeded in reversing decisions to bring cheaper technical solutions to market whenever these had not yet gone through the full testing programme.

Throughout this period my diary commitments were impossible to juggle, as both of my areas of responsibility demanded a lot of face-to-face presence. I felt as if I were living in perpetual shade, as if I were in a submarine: I no longer went out, and my sole sustenance was the files that my driver dropped off at my house – even on Friday evenings to keep me busy over the weekends. It was at this point, when I had no spare time whatsoever, that my executive secretary, Serge Van Hove, persuaded me to take a bit of time to come up for air and to mix with other people. This he did by arranging a series of lunches at which I had the pleasure of sharing my table with people from the wider world: key thinkers such as the Franco-American writer Guy Sorman and the remarkable Pierre Bézier, developer of the famous Bézier curve, used in computer graphics, as well as the transfer machines that did so much to revolutionize the world of manufacturing. There was also François de Closets, who in 1996 published a well-received book on education, *Le bonheur d'apprendre* (the joy of learning); André Essel, co-founder of the Fnac cultural and electronic retail chain, which began as a buyers' club in the 1950s; Joël de Rosnay, a scientist who opened my eyes; Jacques Maillot, founder of travel organization Nouvelles Frontières, who arrived on his scooter; and even the designer Philippe Starck, who showed us his Toto project – '*La toto à Toto*', he said, a baby's car for baby Toto. This made me smile, even though I had a lot of trouble getting Starck to realize that his Citroën Méhari-like ultra-basic car project was not going to become the next Ford Model T.

All these lunches took place in the very chic directors' restaurant, where at the height of the mad cow beef crisis the excellent chef used all his skills to provide us with a menu that was almost exclusively duck – unsurprising, as he was from the southwest of France, where duck is a speciality. And even if, as a result, I will never eat duck again, I still recall those meetings with great pleasure, for the enlightenment they provided me in my role as a designer. They were so very nourishing, and I am still enjoying the benefits today.

Castles made of sand

Whether in sports, art, politics or business, two kinds of people can be found: the ones – let us call them artists – who consider that the greatest of achievement is to do one's best, notwithstanding the level they will attain; and the ones – leaders – who want to be first, whatever it takes and whatever the field they will occupy. In both cases, hazards are numerous. For artists, the idea of going down the hill can be unbearable. The Roman statesman and military leader Lucius Quinctius Cincinnatus returning to his farm; *The Tempest*'s Prospero (and with him Shakespeare) breaking his staff; Gioachino Rossini retiring from composing at the age of 38, to take up cooking: they are mere exceptions, compared to people who keep on performing weaker and weaker renditions of what they once were. For leaders, the idea of relinquishing power can be equally unbearable. In 2018, the premature death of Sergio Marchionne, CEO of Fiat-Chrysler and president of Ferrari, showed how the need for power can ultimately be more important than life: even if not the primary cause of his illness, 20-hour working days (and chain-smoking) certainly played a part. As did, maybe, the idea that he had to step down.

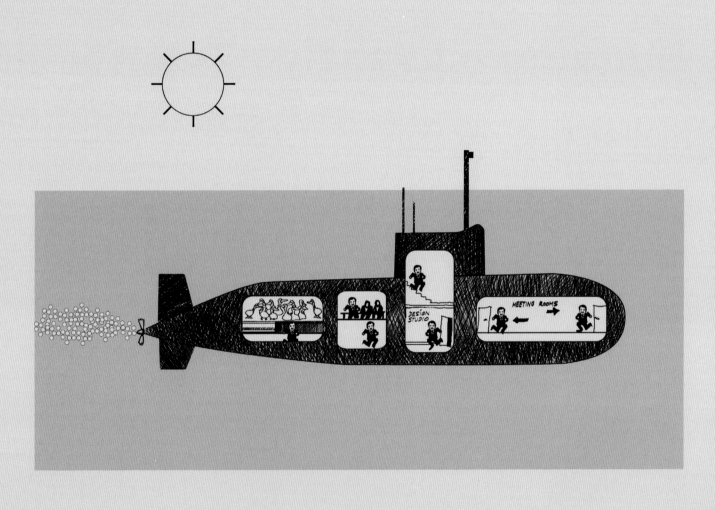

Building a Creative Team

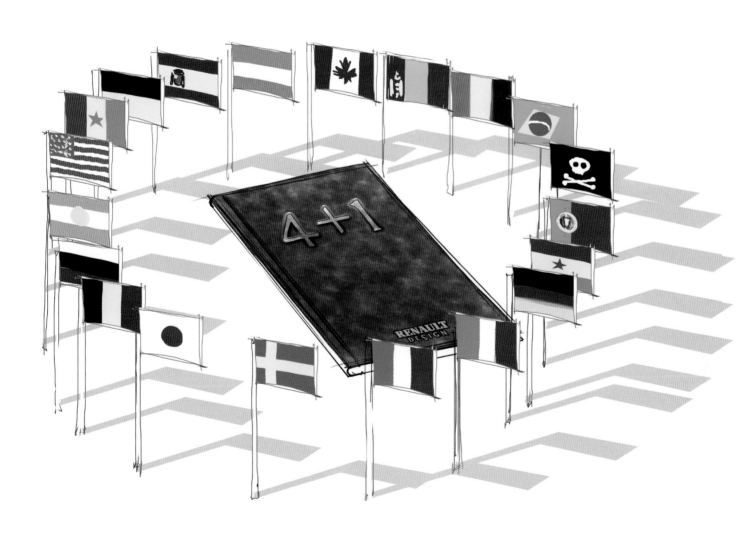

Over the many years and across the different marques where I served as design director, I must have hired several hundred designers – in Europe, in North and South America, and in Asia. My largest team was the one at Renault, where we boasted some 140 designers from twenty-eight different countries, scattered across six design centres around the world. Early on, we established a set of five criteria to assess each new designer hoping to join our ranks. We called them the 4+1, and here they are:

No.1: A passion for design – A designer cannot design unless he or she is totally involved. Designers must live, eat, drink and think design. A designer needs to be curious, enthusiastic and open, for the human brain is like a parachute – it works better when it is open. The design profession is a one-way street: once you've trained as a designer there is no turning back, and you'll never be able to see the world in the same way as before.

No.2: Drawing – I have only ever hired designers who show an exceptionally good mastery of drawing techniques, for drawing is a universal language that enables communication in a multicultural working environment. Drawing is the passport that takes you over every frontier. But take note – it is more than just a means of communication: it can also stimulate the brain to analyze things better, to think more clearly and then to make better choices and develop more effective ideas.

No.3: Empathy – A very important issue for designers is to know how to put themselves into the position of other people, such as customers and operators. This requires awareness, a certain sensitivity and a lot of openness. Empathy is being interested in other people and being able to identify with them, as well as having the ability to imagine how other people might feel and what their needs might be. Intuition is also required, but it must be fed by empathy.

No.4: The team – As I mentioned earlier, Enzo Ferrari, founder of the marque that bears his name, once observed that 'the team has replaced the solitary genius', in effect saying that it is essential to be able to work closely with others, whether as part of a group of designers or within a multidisciplinary team. For designers, no matter how brilliantly intelligent, creative and talented they are, working in isolation will never be an adequate substitute for cross-pollinating ideas with other people, exchanging thoughts on the same subject, coming up with contrasting points of view and sparking creative dialogue.

No.4+1: Talent – And then there is talent. You can have an all-consuming passion for creativity, you can be a master in the art of drawing, you can demonstrate genuine sensitivity and empathy towards others, and you can be a respected member of a team. Yet if you don't have talent, you won't amount to much.

Unfortunately, even having put together a highly talented team is not sufficient to guarantee the sustained output of successful projects: keeping up the momentum is one of the biggest challenges confronting the managers of creative teams. The crucial test is to ensure that the first spectacular success is not immediately followed by a plunge into mediocrity, even fleetingly. Excellence is genuine only when it is permanently inscribed into the culture: the big issue is repeatability.

How can we guard against the loss of creative spark within an organization? There are many factors that come into play here, including the quality of personal relationships based on respect, and the way in which projects are managed – especially when it comes to keeping to an absolute minimum any compromises that might detract from the substance of the project. It is also a question of the quality of the environment and how that might generate a particular atmosphere, because this can also play a significant role in the creativity of a team. But what is most crucial is to introduce fresh stimuli that break up the routine – a routine which, with time, risks anaesthetizing the creatives. And to prevent the group ossifying into a destructive routine, it is equally imperative to continue to question how that group is organized.

Another of our initiatives was to set up meetings with stimulating people, such as the historian and brilliant conference presenter Jean-Louis Loubet, who delivered a series of talks at Renault Design on the history of French cars. We also encouraged the inspiration and cultural enlightenment that come from trend-spotting activities: these missions give designers the chance to 'recharge their batteries' by attending major shows outside the world of the automobile and mixing with other creatives working in different fields; on their return, their experiences are then shared with the rest of the Design team. In this way, four times a year, seven or eight of our designers would go on trend missions to the Milan Furniture Fair, for example, or travel to a large capital city for thought-provoking meetings. They would always return from these trips full of ideas, which they would share with their colleagues through presentations or highly perceptive video shows.

These topics took centre stage in the conversation we had with Steve Jobs, the co-founder of Apple, who visited us at our Paris-Bastille satellite design centre one Saturday morning in 2003. This very special encounter was recorded in a single picture, the only one, taken by the Centre's director, Fabio Filippini: both he and Pascale Bauer, my executive secretary, took part in this impassioned exchange of views. For quite some time we debated the subject of how to keep a team working at the very top of its game, and discussed how we could share our respective methods. What a treat it was to hear Jobs speaking! This was a person who had been thrown out of his own company and who later returned to save it, just as it was close to filing for bankruptcy; and someone who, finally, turned Apple into a global leader and a source of influence for the world's creative community. Thank you, Mr Jobs, for all the inspiration and motivation you have given us.

Labour, divided?

Specialization has become the norm, and division of labour has been considered to be the key to performance since the start of the Industrial Revolution (and even earlier: it was observed and described by the English economist William Petty in Dutch shipyards in the seventeenth century). It is also utilized in design, and especially automotive design, with studios now employing several hundred people, each person dedicated to doing what they are the most skilled at: drafting, modelling, CAD... Although such teamwork is obviously dictated by economic priorities, and especially by the simultaneous work needed to reduce development time, it is also required because of the increasing complexity of cars. Being able to understand the technical issues of a design, to answer them elegantly, and to produce a two-, then a three-dimensional prototype of the proposed solution, requires a set of competences akin to those the Roman architect and engineer Vitruvius expected of fellow architects. Finding all of these in one single person is very difficult. A few characters, however, have managed that feat over the years. Citroën's Flaminio Bertoni could reputedly draw a complete car at night and sculpt a model of it the day after; and to this day Gordon Murray, of Brabham and McLaren fame, remains one of the few people who can design a car in its entirety.

43

Call in the Headhunter

A hunter who has himself been hunted knows better than anyone else how it all works; how to target someone who is not your prey but, rather, your preferred choice. But first a word of explanation to those not familiar with the workings of the corporate world: the headhunter is someone who is tasked by the company to track down an individual at a rival company, with the purpose of organizing a meeting that could subsequently lead to an offer of employment. Typically, the headhunter's role involves finding out the private phone number of the person being targeted, then arranging a time and place for a preliminary meeting – all without any mention of who is behind the request.

My first contact with a headhunter came in early 1987. At the time I was in charge of the Volkswagen-Audi Group design centre in Düsseldorf, Germany, and my future career seemed to be mapped out in front of me as I was set to be named as the very first design director for the whole group, which at that time encompassed the Volkswagen, Audi and Seat brands. This position had been promised to me by the then CEO of Volkswagen, Carl Hahn, when I first met him: a time frame of two years had been given to me when I joined the group and I was reaching the point where my new assignment in Wolfsburg was about to begin. But each day, as the fateful date for moving from our house in Cologne drew nearer, my wife and I found our enthusiasm was ebbing away.

Besides, I had responded positively to overtures for a meeting with members of the BMW board who wanted to hire me as number two in their design department, with the intention of my becoming the eventual successor to Claus Luthe, the great designer who had earlier in his career shaped the remarkable NSU Ro80. And of course Munich, where BMW has its headquarters, was very different from the 'soulless suburb' of Wolfsburg, which is just a stone's throw from what was then East Germany.

I accepted the BMW job but did not fully finalize things because at almost exactly the same time I was contacted by a former deputy director of product planning from Renault, a certain François Wasservogel. Wasservogel arranged for me to meet Renault's president, Raymond Lévy, and even though Renault appeared to be on the brink of bankruptcy I was unable to refuse the offer that was put in front of me.

I had a fantastic first few years at Renault. Although Raymond Lévy retired in 1991, three years after I arrived at the company, he was replaced by the remarkable Louis Schweitzer, with whom I developed a relationship of deep trust, friendship even. By 1995 I had been appointed to the directors' committee, even though I was aware that everything could fall apart from one day to the next and that there was a groundswell of 'antibody' sentiment that rejected anybody from outside the company. To make matters worse, a Polytechnicien candidate (one who had studied at the prestigious École Polytechnique) had been turned down for Director of Styling, the position that I was given. Even in 1998, when I was contacted by a headhunter working on behalf of Mercedes-Benz to find a replacement for the legendary design director Bruno Sacco, I thought hard but still finally said no: I had decided that my family life would stay centred in France and nowhere else.

Come 1999, the hunted turned hunter: following the formation of the Renault-Nissan Alliance I was given the task of auditing Nissan Design, an organization that had shone brilliantly in the early 1990s but which had stagnated badly since then. My mission was two-fold: firstly, to get to the bottom of the reasons for this meltdown and inform the Renault leadership; and secondly, to find a new person to lead Nissan Design. So I looked carefully through the list of the best designers that I knew, designers who could also speak both Japanese and English, and came up with three names; these I passed to a headhunter based in New York. The New York organization

Left to right: Shiro Nakamura, Patrick le Quément and Carl Hahn.

put forward a few more names, too, but none of them seemed suitable to me.

Meetings were arranged in New York for me to speak to each of the contenders, the whole thing very carefully timetabled to ensure that no candidate could ever meet another one in the lift. I had saved the best candidate, Shiro Nakamura, for last: for quite some time I had been following his career as design director at Isuzu, thinking that, perhaps, one day…. My plan thus allowed me to continue our discussions over a meal; my report consisted of a single recommendation, Carlos Ghosn (president of Nissan at the time) interviewed him and it was Shiro Nakamura who was appointed. In his autobiography, *Citoyen du monde* (2003; Citizen of the world), Ghosn even went as far as expressing his gratitude to me for this.

My last experience in the role of hunter was in response to a task conferred on me by the man who had become my new boss at Renault, Carlos Ghosn – to find my own successor. There was just one rule: I was first to put forward the names of two internal candidates, then I was to propose a single candidate from outside the company. This time I chose a Paris-based headhunting agency, giving them three names to approach. Almost immediately I was able to make my recommendation. Patrick Pélata, who was head of the Renault brand at the time, interviewed all three candidates, but only Laurens van den Acker, who was at Mazda, succeeded in getting through and meeting Ghosn.

As I remember it, there was one fundamental question about Laurens that worried Ghosn: 'Isn't he too young to take on such a level of responsibility?' he asked me. Without hesitation I replied: 'Laurens is the same age I was when I took charge of Renault Design.' That's how everything was settled, and I could now move on to other ventures. Mission accomplished!

Designated survivors

Big companies are a bit like Broadway productions: the show must go on whatever happens, even if some members of the cast are reported missing. For years, the human resources policy of Renault was based on the 'bus accident theory': an executive always had a duly identified potential stand-in, should an accident such as being run over by a bus occur. Things are not as easy to manage where company presidents are concerned. Sometimes they are reluctant to step off, and even more so to organize their succession. Peugeot's Jacques Calvet remained in his office and performed his duties up to the last minute of the last day, as if nothing was going to happen. Naturally, he had not wanted to take an active part in the search that led to the (excellent) choice of Jean-Martin Folz. Then too, the necessary competences of a candidate are very hard to define: 'serial CEOs' who go from one company to the other do not necessarily understand the specifics of the automotive industry; great car people are sometimes not-so-great managers; and occasionally, some people who were initially neither, such as Citroën's Pierre-Jules Boulanger or Renault's Pierre Dreyfus, can be great leaders of the industry.

44

Design Takes to the Water

The last few months leading up to my departure from Renault in October 2009 were so intense that I was unable to snatch a single moment to myself to think about what I wanted to do afterwards. Aside from the word itself, the concept of 'retirement' held no allure for me – and, besides, I had far too much to do! Right up to the very last minute I had been focused on a crucial task: finding someone to take over from me as head of Renault Design. It was a difficult mission, but a stimulating one, too – and all the more satisfying as the handover to Laurens van den Acker was particularly pleasant. One way or another, and for him as much as for me, the baton needed to be passed on; so I decided that I would step right back as soon as I possibly could, after I had shown Laurens round all the studios and workshops, introduced him to all the teams, reviewed all the ongoing projects with him and attended all the major scheduled company meetings.

So for the rest of my time at Renault I stayed upstairs in my office. Was that easy? Of course not. I was entrusting Laurens with many projects that were close to my heart: the Zoe, very nearly ready for a silent electric launch and, most particularly, the new Clio IV. Shaped by a young and talented designer, Yann Jarsallé, the design proposal had stunned me, and I was overjoyed that this project also became a favourite of my successor. Almost three years later, just after the Clio IV's market launch, I sent a message of congratulations to Jean-Pierre Barlog, the Design project manager. And this is how Jean-Pierre replied: 'Yes, the Clio has been a great story, but rather than imagining that your memory is failing you, I think you've had the grace to forget that it was you who selected the right design.' It was a wrench to leave those projects, and there were some regrets, but the success of the Zoe and the Clio IV in the years that followed continues to be a source of great satisfaction to me.

A month before I left Renault I was contacted by Xavier Desmarest. He is one of the founders of Grand Large Yachting, a venture which brought together under the same umbrella several companies in the field of sailing yachts; one of these, Outremer, specializes in building ocean-going catamarans. Xavier had picked up on press reports that I was about to leave Renault, and he was interested in my experience as a former director of quality, a responsibility I had held at the automaker for four years. Acutely aware that as far as the client is concerned there are never any second chances to make a good first impression, he was hoping that I could apply my know-how to help improve the perceived quality of his boats. It was a time of crisis for me, too, so I was interested. Most of all, though, I felt the need to pick up my pencils once more: much like a virtuoso violinist who had enjoyed a long career conducting an orchestra, I wanted to play my own instrument again. And it was just at the moment when I was beginning to re-bond with my pencils that Xavier asked to see me again.

We met up during one of his trips to Paris; the majority of his time is spent at La Grande Motte where the Outremer craft are built, on the Mediterranean coast near Montpellier. Straight away he asked if I would join the 'dream team' that he had put together to handle the exterior design of their upcoming flagship vessel, the Outremer 5X. The dream team consisted of the interior designer Franck Darnet and the highly regarded naval architecture practice VPLP, led by Marc Van Peteghem and Vincent Lauriot-Prévost.

I had already met the VPLP people in 2000, when Renault Design took part in the Concept Cat project for an experimental catamaran. Being able to work with Marc once again was a double bonus for me, so of course I took on the challenge. And that was how I came to start work as an apprentice in a discipline that I knew nothing about – for despite my many years of experience in car design, the world of boats was entirely new to me. This marked the start of my association with one of the top firms of naval architects: VPLP is globally

The Outremer 5X.

renowned for its huge catamarans, such as Douce France and Hémisphère, as well as the range of boats from Lagoon – an excellent firm and the world's largest builder of sailboats. And, last but not least, VPLP is famous for its high-performance sailing yachts.

So, how did I fare in this new and unexpected world? As a first step I began to assess the parallels with automotive design, and to adapt the methods and the stages of the creative process, one by one: understanding the 'DNA' of the brand in question, then deciding on the three or four key messages that encapsulate the quintessential qualities the brand is aiming for. Then it is important to ensure a close working relationship with the architects in order to achieve harmonious proportions so that, finally, a design theme can be developed that reflects the desired brand DNA. Next comes the digital 3D design phase where, in sharp contrast to car practice, no fullsize proposals or scale models are built: everything is done on the screen. This makes it imperative to have the right kind of software and, above all, to find a digital design ace who can finely polish the fluidity of all the lines and finesse the quality of the volumes, while also bearing in mind the baseline priorities of practicality and functional efficiency. The process can often be strongly reminiscent of a game of table tennis, as the 'ball' is batted back and forth between the shipyard's design office on the one hand and the architects and the designer on the other. This is the type of dialogue that I would describe as the rubbing of antennae between people who think with their heads and those who think with their hearts.

The Outremer 5X was launched in 2013 and was declared European Yacht of the Year, and in 2014 it was voted Multihull of the Year in the United States.

Still waters run deep (1)

For ages, boats made people dream, conveying images of adventure and freedom. Hence, it was inevitable that boat design would at times provide inspiration for car design, and vice versa: fitting a boat with an internal combustion engine was done for the first time in 1886, and was the idea of a certain Gottlieb Daimler; conversely, one of the most iconic types of car bodies invented in Italy is the Barchetta, which in Italian means 'small boat'. So, the connections are numerous. But more difficult to understand are the many attempts to produce roadworthy boats, or maybe seaworthy cars. Although in 2004 Virgin supremo Richard Branson managed to cross the English Channel with an amphibious vehicle in 1 hour, 40 minutes and 6 seconds, most such vehicles have been rather unsatisfactory, if picturesque, devices, starting with the first of them, the 1805 steam-powered Oruktor Amphibolos by the American inventor Oliver Evans. Although it qualifies as the first American car, it probably never could move under its own power, either on land or in the water. For a century at least, the only category of people showing real interest in amphibious vehicles has been the military, which in itself might lead to real doubts.

Design Takes to the Water

45

My Two Passions

Ever since I was a child, two great passions have ruled my life: cars and design. And when, in late 2009, the moment came for me to leave the automobile industry, I realized that my existence would be turned upside down. I had been design director for a succession of marques for several decades, and I knew that there would suddenly be a great void in my life, as if I had lost one of my limbs.

But even though I received several offers, I did not make any effort to stay in this industry, wonderful and inspiring though it is. I had no desire to seek out a backstage role as a consultant for a Chinese automaker: for me, having to be in the jump seat to remain in the industry – as so many have done – was too great a price to pay. Nor did I fancy (as was actually offered to me) being part of a team commissioned to map out the ultimate supercar – *bolides* (fireballs), as the French say, whose sole mission is to accelerate a fraction of a second quicker than the most recent of these automotive monsters to have reached the market. They offer insane and absurd blast-offs from nought to nowhere, as practised en masse over a few metres between the Casino and the Hotel de Paris by most of the supercars domiciled in Monte Carlo.

I had stepped back, once and for all, from all my work as a designer of cars, yet from the outset I could feel the desire to get back to my drawing board. In order to do that, however, I had to re-learn the art of drawing. Of course I was still capable of producing a quick explanatory sketch, something that others might call a rough, but for many years I had not done any drawing for actual presentations. So I began devoting several hours of each day to drawing; this went on for several long months, after which – what joy! – I had rediscovered my drawing skills. Once again, I was able to put onto paper whatever ideas came into my head, and I could let my hand be my guide to discover things that I did not realize I was looking for. The great painter Pierre Soulages came up with an intriguing

thought, the wording of which I have adapted slightly to suit my argument: 'Whatever I find helps me to learn what I am looking for.'

What this suggests is that drawing is sometimes a medium, a means of transmission that transcends the conscious and which allows instinct to roam free until the process of analysis gains the upper hand. I have often noticed that, while sketching, my first few rough and exploratory lines are the ones I keep returning to as I go deeper into the project. Interestingly, I recently came across much the same sentiment when reading *Designing for People* (1955) by Henry Dreyfuss, one of the most celebrated industrial designers of the 1930s and 1940s and a contemporary of Raymond Loewy, father of the sublime 1953 Studebaker Commander hardtop. Something of a work of reference in the field of industrial design, the book details the design of the legendary Western Electric model 302 telephone for the Bell company, for which the design teams produced some 2500 drawings. Dreyfuss made this observation: 'Curiously, as I have noticed in the past, it was the very first sketch which they ended up focusing on.'

After I had established which activities I no longer wanted to pursue, an opportunity dropped into my lap, as if by remarkable chance: designing a large ocean-going sailing catamaran. For me it was the perfect introduction to the subject, and I soon discovered that, just as in the area of automobiles, 130 years young but still using vocabulary drawn from the horse and cart, the world of sailboats spoke in its own exotic thousand year-old language – a language as alien as Latvian would be to someone of Latin descent. One example springs to mind: on a car, the line at the base of the side windows is known as the waistline or beltline. In French naval architecture this is termed 'tas du rouf' or, literally, the pile of the deckhouse.

Yet, despite all this linguistic trial and error I quickly found my bearings when it came to design. Of course a 20-metre yacht seems pretty big to someone who is accustomed to working on vehicle designs that are never more than 5 metres in length, but the quest for perfect proportions is still an absolute imperative: having the right proportions is the foundation for everything. Boats are designed from the inside out so as to offer the best possible interior space. Next the designer needs to ensure that all the exterior character lines flow smoothly; this is important as the acceleration of a line when it meets a radius, allied to the sculptural quality of a surface, can express either power or solidity, or even lightness, depending on the priorities set by the manufacturer. And it is here that the designer is in his or her element, whether the product is a family car, a toaster, an excavator or a boat.

Nowadays, although I still continue to feast my eyes on fabulous older cars as a jury member at *concours d'élégance* events such as the Villa d'Este (see page 192), it is my latest challenges that inspire me as I get up each morning and that provide pleasure lasting the whole day long. These are my boat projects, the smallest of which is 11 metres and the largest well over 50 metres in length, nearly all of them designed in collaboration with my architect friends at the VPLP agency.

To date, I have designed some thirty sailboats, with more than 1100 examples built. That figure might appear quite high, but it pales into insignificance when compared to the sixty million vehicles I have been associated with over my forty-two years as an automotive designer. I have calculated that, placed bumper-to-bumper behind one another, this line of vehicles would circle the earth some 6438 times. I still retain the same passion for design and for creativity that I always had, and I still have the same terror of the blank page that haunts every designer at night. And I can assure you that every single one of my boat projects has been designed with just as much care and attention to detail as I gave to the projects I delivered across my entire *œuvre* of automotive programmes.

Still waters run deep (2)

If amphibious vehicles remain more of a curiosity than anything else, there is a more significant link between cars and boats. Or rather there are two links: speed and style. Driving a speedboat, although it requires a specific technique, provides analogous thrills to driving a racing car. Indeed, they often have a technical relationship, as shown by the 1953 Timossi Ferrari Arno XI, a racing boat propelled by a Ferrari Formula One engine. Between the 1930s and the 1960s, the likes of Henry Segrave, Kaye Don, Malcolm and Donald Campbell and John Cobb tried to break speed records both on land and on water, and often succeeded. But lakes can be even more lethal than racetracks: Segrave, Donald Campbell and Cobb eventually died in their boats, as did former French racing driver Didier Pironi during an offshore race in 1987. Hopefully, the connections between boat and car design are less tragic: since the 1950s, the Italian Riva yachts have often been compared to Ferraris, not of the racing kind but more the glamorous sort, both being favoured by 'beautiful people' (Alain Delon, Peter Sellers and Gianni Agnelli all owned Ferraris and Rivas) coolly showing off either on the shores or on the glistening surface of the Italian lakes.

46
Villa d'Este

Villa d'Este! When I pronounce that name in a Marcello Mastroianni accent I'm straight through the first portal and into the part of a deeply ingrained fantasy: Mastroianni at the wheel of a Ferrari 250 GT SWB California, with Sophia Loren by his side. But the Villa d'Este hotel, in Cernobbio in northern Italy, is also the place where the world's most glamorous automobile *concours d'élégance* takes place every year; the competition's origins stretch back to 1929, and it has been hosted by BMW since 1999. What is more, it provides a visual feast of the topmost quality, paying homage to decades of exquisite coachwork – and of course showing that Italy, even when it was ruled by that comic-opera dictator Benito Mussolini, knew how to design not only beautiful cars but also magnificent uniforms. This is one of the many talents of that country and one that, even today, allows a humble *carabinieri* to have the allure of a field marshal in the army rather than of a hotel porter.

And with Villa d'Este it is not just the charm of its Lake Como setting but also that of the hotel itself, with its architecture that dates back to 1568: in 2015 it was voted the best hotel in the world. The 'villa' was built for a senior figure in the Church, Cardinal Tomeo Gallio, yet it immediately makes me think of *la dolce vita*. Sorry, Monseigneur!

I joined the jury in 1997. In my first three years it was presided over by a legendary figure: Carlo Anderloni, who had revived Carrozzeria Touring, the design house founded by his father in 1926 and which ran until its closure in 1966 (see boxed text overleaf). Touring has always been one of my favourites among the Italian *carrozzerie*, and its 1939 Alfa Romeo 6C 2500 deserves a place among world automotive heritage nobility. I love it for its breathtaking lines, for its volumes that are ample yet still taut, and for proportions so cleverly conceived to give an air of being powerfully propelled.

Since my first year at Villa d'Este I have had the privilege of rubbing shoulders with some of the great figures of the automobile universe: among these was the renowned Count Albrecht von Goertz, designer of the BMW 507. To my surprise he professed himself a big fan of the Twingo – the first-generation model, of course, and the one I had immediately called the 'instinctive' one (see page 76). Every year he called me to ask when the next Twingo was going to come out and, thank goodness, he passed away at the age of ninety-two, before the delayed launch of the second generation: the one that had generated clinic results you would expect from a car designed to not displease, a depressing approach if ever there was one.

In 2004 Lorenzo Ramaciotti took over from Carlo Anderloni as president of the jury. As the former head of design at Pininfarina and, later, Fiat Chrysler, Lorenzo was unanimously appreciated both by successive juries and by the organizers. The two of us are the longest-serving members of the jury, and in this role we share the same desire to rid ourselves of the burden of worrying about how people might react to our decisions, while at the same time retaining an absolute respect for history. Together, we managed to help the jury move on from the idea, firmly instilled in the minds of some members, that only a pre-war car could win a *concours d'élégance*. I remember lengthy debates between jurors before we were able to come up with a majority that first time.

Then we came up against another belief, that only cars with engines of six cylinders or more could be considered eligible for the top prize. Yet in 2017 it was a petite Alfa Romeo Giulietta SS Prototipo of 1957 that took the Best of Show title, the Trofeo BMW Group. Designed by Franco Scaglione, who worked for the Bertone studio at the time, this little gem was the result of his research into aerodynamic efficiency. With a drag

The Ferrari 250 GT SWB California of Patrick le Quément's Mastroianni fantasy.

coefficient (C_d) of only 0.28 and a weight of a mere 800 kg thanks to aluminium bodywork, it had a 1.3 litre four-cylinder engine developing 100 horsepower – enough to reach the 120 mph mark. It is a benchmark for lightness, something close to many hearts in France (see page 149).

After the jury had made its decision, some members were concerned as to what the public would choose on the Sunday afternoon; the 'Best of Show' awarded by the jury would not be announced until the gala dinner that same evening. After all, we had chosen a car that, with very few modifications, reappeared as a production model, the Giulietta Sprint Speciale, and enjoyed a production run of 1350 units. Had we underrated the importance of exclusivity? To our astonishment the public prize that afternoon went to the Alfa Romeo, too.

Which goes to show that we must never underestimate real and genuine passion for cars. As they say, *Vox populi, vox Dei* – the voice of the people is the voice of God.

Touring

Touring is less known today than Pininfarina or Bertone, maybe because it disappeared quite early, in 1966. However, its forty-year life left a durable mark, thanks to its wonderfully balanced designs and to its permanent quest for lightness and innovation. Lightness was not a given, though. Touring's founder, Felice Bianchi Anderloni, was closely linked to Isotta Fraschini, which was known for extremely refined and extremely heavy cars (Anderloni's three sisters had respectively married Cesare Isotta, Antonio Fraschini and Vincenzo Fraschini). Still, Touring quickly started producing bodies using the lightweight but complex Weymann patent, before introducing in 1937 its own Superleggera ('superlight') technique, consisting of aluminium bodies on a cage of welded small-diameter steel tubes. Its success was immediate, and led to several era-defining bodies, particularly on Alfa Romeo chassis. After World War II, when demand remained high for exclusive, limited series, Touring carried on working for Alfa Romeo, and for the likes of Lancia, Maserati, Lamborghini and Aston Martin, before closing. However, the brand was not to be forgotten, and was revived in 2006. The 'new' Touring has since produced striking concepts, the most recent being the 2018 Maserati Sciadipersia. And, in 2018, Aston Martin decided to revive the Superleggera name on some of its future models.

47

The Embalmers:
A Restoration Comedy

Preserving the automotive heritage is as much about the men and women behind the vehicles as about the physical upkeep of the wonderful creations themselves. This legacy is safeguarded not only through museums set up by manufacturers to maintain their own histories, but also through independent museums and by clubs and associations that keep the legend alive by rescuing examples of automotive art from oblivion – including models that some might regard as insignificant. It has also become a full-scale business in its own right, with auction houses feeding the market and helping to inflate the values of these exceptional cars. And, finally, there are *concours d'élégance* events, which give the broader public the chance to see the finest specimens populating the automotive history books.

Preserving our industrial heritage is a noble endeavour, whether it relates to artefacts from the railways or those connected to the weaving industry. This reminds me of a museum I have visited on many occasions and which always impressed me with the quality of its resources and its scene setting: the Henry Ford Museum of American Innovation in Dearborn, a suburb of Detroit. This museum has everything: cars, of course, but also railway locomotives, agricultural implements, tools, machinery – it is a veritable treasure trove on a grand scale and feels truly authentic, right down to the way the cars are placed within their period settings. It is a million miles away from how most collectors' cars tend to be preserved, for the great predominance of American collectors in the 1970s gave rise to a disturbing phenomenon, over-restoration.

This tendency was probably exacerbated by the influence of George Barris, known as Mr Chrome and celebrated on the US West Coast as the king of customization. Designer and builder of the 1966–68 Batmobile, Barris was immortalized by the American writer Tom Wolfe in his remarkable book *The Kandy-Kolored Tangerine-Flake Streamline Baby* (1965). This was an era when there was great interest in preserving beautiful cars, even if the restorations were all too often excessive and painted a false picture of the period in which the vehicles were built. This was true enough for normal road cars, but it was even more blatant when it came to racing machinery, which could sometimes resemble dolled-up poodles emerging from a grooming parlour.

When I first began to take part in European *concours d'élégance* events at the end of the 1980s, the members of the European judging panels were by and large wise to this phenomenon of rewriting history. At the series of Louis Vuitton Classic competitions held between 1988 and 2002, jury president Christian Philippsen underlined the importance of authenticity, reminding us that automobiles were first and foremost a means of transport – and not sculptures created from scratch and mounted on top of a marble plinth (see also page 144). So we hailed a succession of cars whose paintwork and general patina would have ruled them out of most of the American events taking place at that time.

In 2002, uplifted by our crusade-like wave of enthusiasm for authenticity, the Louis Vuitton Classic jury even went so far as very nearly awarding the top prize to a 1906 Renault VI Torpedo presented in its original – unrestored – condition. This vehicle, driven by a tough old cookie, had stayed in the same family's ownership since it was new, and its shape haunts me to this day: tall and imposing and with nightmarish proportions, and the windscreen and its hood combined to create the impression of a Basque beret. It was a close-run thing but in the end common sense prevailed and the elderly Renault was denied the top step of the podium, even though it did win its own category. And on the day the overall Best in Show award went to a splendid Ferrari 250 MM dating from 1953.

A number of years later I found myself in the company of several fellow design directors – both active and retired – from different automakers, at a *concours d'élégance* in Bergerac, in the Périgord in western France.

The Maserati A6G 2000 Gran Sport Berlinetta.

The competition had been organized by a former colleague, Claude Lobo, and the president of the jury was Uwe Bahnsen, my one-time director of design at Ford of Europe. Part of the programme saw all the participants head out, at the controls of priceless automotive masterpieces from Bugatti, Voisin, Facel Vega, Bentley and more, to visit an automobile museum at the ancient Château de Sanxet. The museum houses a very eclectic collection of rare cars, but on our visit all of them were in a dreadful state and clearly rotting away rapidly. Quite a few of us had trouble sleeping that night, dismayed by the squandering of our heritage that we had just witnessed. It was akin to a death sentence through neglect for a set of unusual cars that included a 1935 Panhard & Levassor 6 CS RL-N Coupé, designed by Louis Bionier and characterized by its small, well-rounded vertical windows flanking the main windscreen which was, by contrast, quite flat.

In the same way, my heart momentarily skipped a beat when, one day in 2017, I spotted the sublime 1956 Maserati A6G Gran Sport Berlinetta from the former Baillon collection. It was at the *concorso d'eleganza* at Villa d'Este in Italy (see page 192) and was being presented untouched in its barn-find condition. I immediately began wondering: were we witnessing the dawn of a new era in which unscrupulous dealers set about vandalizing collectors' cars in order to push up prices? For me it brought back uncomfortable echoes of the late twentieth-century Benetton advertising campaign art-directed by the great Italian photographer Oliviero Toscani and showing a man dying from AIDS, stretched out on a bed and surrounded by his close family and friends.

Ladies and gentlemen of the classic-car collector world, please bring back dignity to our vehicles. They may belong to you right now, but they will always be part of our collective automotive heritage.

To protect and to serve

There are car collectors, and there are car lovers. A few people are both, but what is the difference between them? Car lovers love cars as cars, that is to mean mobile objects, which in addition can be remarkably beautiful, or sophisticated, or powerful, or whatever qualities they are possessed with (or not: there are Austin Allegro fanatics). They want to use their cars, even if (and sometimes because) it implies incessantly tinkering with them, and accepting that, like a well-worn jacket, they show traces of use. On the other hand, collectors, of cars, stamps, watches or whatever, want to stop time. They need to keep things under control, with the underlying thought that using something depreciates it. Whether over-restored, lovingly preserved, or left in various states of decay, their cars must be as numerous as possible (which, unless it is a full-time occupation, precludes using them), and preferably must never move under their own power. When in 2015 a few journalists were allowed a brief drive in the Baillon 'barn-find' 1961 Ferrari 250 GT California, they were asked to be careful not to disturb the dust on the car's derelict body.

The Embalmers: A Restoration Comedy

48

Ali Baba's Caves

As it turned out, I didn't need to know the password to get into Ali Baba's cave – and I was never in any danger of the forty thieves coming back to finish me off. It all began with this mysterious message: 'I want to make you an offer: come and visit Ali Baba's cave next Saturday. It's in a secret location not far from XYZ. Believe me, you'll really love it.'

This was how I was approached by my friend Renaud Tourte with the offer of going to meet up with one of my former designers. HA, as we will call him, was a glittering talent who, well before I came to Renault Design, and while he was still a trainee, shaped the very first Clio. Today, he runs his own organization and has acquired a building in which he houses and looks after his collection of cars as well as those of his friends, the great majority of whom are also car designers. We spent the morning strolling among a host of rare cars as he talked us through his personal history as well as the stories behind each car – its origins, its special features. There were Porsches, several Ferraris, three Jaguar E-Types and three Lamborghinis, the very earliest of which was the car he drove to work every day when he first started at Renault Design. And there were Maseratis, a Morgan and a Chevrolet Corvette – and more too.

In the midst of this marvellous treasure trove I came across one of the cars owned by HA's family, a car that had stayed walled up in a garage in his home country for thirty-five years as he waited for permission from the local authorities to release the vehicle and take it to France. This 1950s Mercedes 300SL convertible is a car that comes close to automotive perfection, its intrinsic beauty intimately bound up with its timeless proportions. And although this particular example was still in unrestored condition, I failed to find even the slightest evidence of the ravages of time on its storm-grey metallic paintwork or in its interior, finished in leather of a subtle greeny turquoise with a hint of grey. The 300SL was placed alongside a superb Jaguar E-Type, and opening and closing the doors of each of them provided an elegant demonstration of the deep-down quality of the Mercedes. Of course this was a Mercedes whose price when launched was twice as much as the Jaguar's – but even so.... With the one, we were treated to a discreetly muffled sound that immediately inspired confidence; with the other, it was the sound of rattling pots and pans that reminded me of a Simca 1100. My hunger satisfied, I left at the end of the morning with a smile on my face.

It was a car-shaped smile and one that returned a month later near Cassis, where I live. Another friend, Pierre-Henry Mahul, who I first met when we were both members of France's Association Sportive Automobile, invited me and several others to dinner at his superb house near Le Castellet by the south coast of France, where the Paul Ricard circuit is located. After the meal I had the happy surprise of discovering that my friend had built an extension to the house, for his business as a trader in collectors' cars. Another Ali Baba's cave!

At first sight, his twenty-odd cars came across as an eclectic collection, and this they certainly were. But what struck me most vividly was the breadth of his automotive vision, which put me in mind of the Irish poet and playwright Oscar Wilde: 'I am a man of simple tastes – I am always satisfied with the best.' In this instance 'the best' could be translated as unique, interesting, having a distinctive character or history – something perhaps reflected in the 1960s Panhard 24CT, itself (like so many other models at that time) inspired in no small measure by the Chevrolet Corvair. Designed by René Ducassou-Pehau under the direction of his boss, Louis Bionier, the 24CT was a real masterpiece: an elegant thoroughbred, it was also notable for its attention to the minutest details – well ahead of the industry practice of the time. And, still with Panhard, a rare 1960s station wagon version of the PL17 was a further surprise.

Pierre-Henry Mahul
in his Morgan Plus
4 Tourer.

There were several Morgans, too, long-standing and faithful friends, Pierre-Henry's favourite being an impressive four-seater Tourer with a 3-litre V6. I also spotted a red CG 1300, the now-forgotten missing link to that other compact coupé, the Alpine A110. The little CG, with its Simca engine, is charming, but for me it stirred up a very particular memory: the response I was given several decades ago by the two men who owned CG, after I had offered them my services as a designer. 'But we don't need any help – we know how to do it', they told me.

There was also a Jaguar E-Type, fitted with broader 8-inch-wide wire spoke wheels. These had the very welcome effect of slightly reducing the E-Type's perennial problem, that of its wheels being set too far inside its wheel arches. Right alongside it was a distinguished Ferrari 456 GT, a model that I have always much admired and whose cabin is the perfect embodiment of refined and high-class interior design in the mid-1990s. In fact, we at Renault brought in a 456 as a reference car during the design process for our Talisman concept car, which explored the theme of simplicity. Another car to catch my eye was my friend's Salmson S4 E cabriolet of 1950 – something from a different era, for sure, but a post-war design that nevertheless projected a certain panache. And then there was a somewhat disturbing 1960 Panhard CD, complete with teardrop tail and catfish mouth – though without the whiskers. Finally, there was a Lancia Aurelia B20 Series IV, made in 1955 and finished in a deep 'misty' red described as Rosso Corsa. With its characteristically tiny, minimalist rear lights, this is a car that I first glimpsed as a child on the Promenade des Anglais in Nice, and which I have admired ever since.

My very special visits to these two 'caves' allowed me to see everything, with nothing missed out. But I still feel the need to return to Ali Baba's two caverns of wonder – and this time I've promised myself I will keep my eyes open still wider, right to the very last car.

Keep it to yourself

Whether or not we consider that cars are meant for being driven, car collectors are vital, as with any form of human creation, to preserve traces of what was once achieved in design and technology. But, like art collectors, they can be either reclusive or eager to share their treasures. Charles G Renaud, a Swiss banker who died in 2006, had accumulated a collection of about 150 cars that he was happy to open to visits and even sometimes to test drives. Others, like the English businessman Tom Wheatcroft (d. 2009) or the US casino magnate Bill Harrah (d. 1978), even opened museums to let the public admire their cars. However, that kind of collector is much rarer than the secretive ones who do not want to show their possessions, let alone allow a magazine to photograph or, worse, drive them: this author remembers one who had to be approached exclusively through his lawyer for months, before he eventually rejected the idea of an article on his collection of one-off Lamborghinis. But the most famous example of collectors keeping it all for themselves remains the Franco-Swiss Schlumpf brothers, who gathered a fabulous collection of Bugattis, built a lavish museum to house them, and never opened it to anyone. Incidentally, their folly also bankrupted their family business.

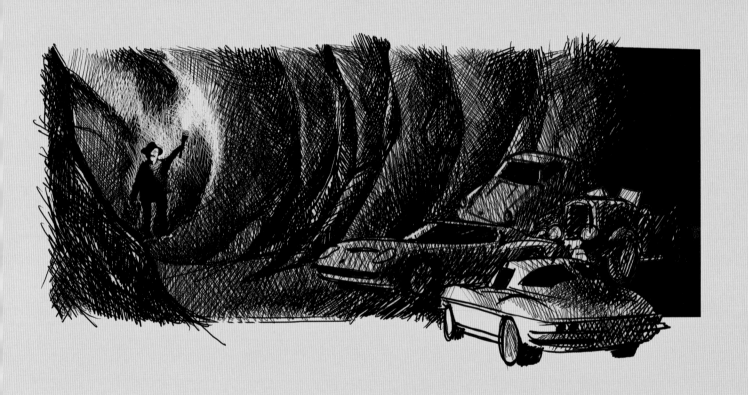

49

Beyond Group-think Uniformity

'Birds of a feather flock together' is a saying that applies not just to wildlife but also to the composition of design teams, whether they are made up of just a handful of designers or several hundred. When we were interviewing for new designers it was clear to me that we would invariably end up asking ourselves the question, 'will he or she fit in smoothly into the team?' But what we never asked ourselves was this: 'will he or she smash the cocoon of calm contentment that the team has built up around itself?'

We are always striving to integrate people, to build constructive relationships and well-knit teams, and to seek harmony and balance. Yet it is important to understand that, even when it comes to aesthetics, and counter to generally accepted opinion, beauty is not achieved by striking the perfect balance. Instead, it stems from a certain imbalance, from something that prompts a reaction and makes it impossible to be indifferent to the object. It is clear, therefore, that in teams in which the overriding priority of the internal culture is to ensure a quiet life rather than taking the risk of developing new ideas, this can only result in uniformity and blandness.

So even though the prevailing attitude tends to lend support to the notion that 'birds of a feather flock together', my years in the creative business have taught me that the inverse also holds true – that those who come together end up resembling one another. I have always pushed for the hiring of free radicals: some describe them as 'bad boys' and 'difficult women', but in any group with a strong sense of belonging there is a need for controlled chaos, too, so as to tip the group into a stimulating creative impulse.

And another thought, which also goes against the grain of received wisdom: how best to ensure the collaborative contribution of every member of a team? How do you make a group work together for maximum creativity? What is needed is both to brainstorm in a group setting, and also to allow everyone to work alone for a length of time so as to

encourage the cultivation of ideas that are different or disruptive, instead of restricting the thinking only to outcomes predetermined by the practices and procedures of a group. And then, rather than rushing too quickly into a single solution, there should be time for reflection, just as it is not a good thing to always be working under time pressure. Or, to put it a different way, you can't make flowers grow faster by pulling on them.

The real enemy of creativity is having too much uniformity among people who work together, who eat together, who do their shopping in the same stores, who read the same books and who rely on the same sources of information. In this way, their similarities gradually become greater than their differences. That's a very real danger, and it is important to watch out for this 'birds of a feather' group-think uniformity.

The warning applies to any creative organization. The creative process is a form of communication, but it is also a preparedness not to communicate: it is an opening up, but it can also be a deliberate cutting off. In 1983 one of France's Academicians and national treasures, the eminent anthropologist and ethnologist Claude Lévi-Strauss, took up this point in a book entitled *Le Regard éloigné* (*The View from Afar*): 'When successful, communication with the other person damages, whether in the short or longer term, the originality of their or my creation.' And this was well before globalization had become such a cause for concern and unrest. So, how are we best to shape the creative contribution of each individual within a collaborative environment without stifling everyone's creative capacity? How to stand up against a phenomenon that seems such an inevitable part of corporate culture? For me, these are among the fundamental questions that the management of creativity poses.

When I switched from the world of automotive design to that of naval architecture I found myself among teams that were just as motivated and just as passionate as the

Left to right:
VPLP's Marc Van Peteghem and Mathias Maurios, Patrick le Quément, Lagoon's Bruno Belmont and Martina Torrini, and VPLP's Marc Dognin.

ones I had left. The VPLP naval architecture consultancy designs boats for clients including Lagoon, the world's leading manufacturer of sailboats; at Lagoon I discovered a very different vision of collective creativity, something that filled important gaps in my own experience and to a large extent responded to the questions I had been asking myself.

First of all, though, let us take a closer look at the specifics of the working relationships between a highly regarded agency, VPLP, its team, its boss, Marc Van Peteghem, and one of Lagoon's senior managers, Bruno Belmont – himself also a naval architect who trained at the same school at Southampton in the UK. The relationship is based on the trust that has built up over the years through regular exchanges – a bit like a constant table tennis – taking place between all the protagonists. Initially, the work is individual, but it is also shared in exchanges with those working in the 'hive', and with others; these people are sometimes based dozens or hundreds of miles away and can bring a wholly different view, independent from that of the group. Naturally, and extending the bee metaphor, they return to the hive on a regular basis to 'rub antennae', then fly off again, each with a fresh stimulus to their imagination. In general, an idea is put forward and is often taken up by others in order to be finally steered through by… everyone? Next, there follows a period of non-communication, its purpose being to allow all the parties the time to think independently by themselves before sharing again. The digital age is officially with us: it allows us to rethink our ways of working in groups – and this is only the beginning.

As for me, I like working within a group where I don't need to be careful to be careful. I like working in a setting where everyone recognizes the need to provide time for time itself, but also where at a given moment you have to have all hands on deck to achieve the final objective as fast as possible – the market simply won't wait. Any idea, even the most brilliant, remains a product of the era in which we live. As soon as an idea is formed, it needs to mature, and then be put into practice before others have the chance to get ahead of you with it. And, as the avant-garde early-twentieth-century artist Francis Picabia so aptly noted, 'the only way to be ahead is to run faster than the others.'

Chalk and cheese

Differences and disagreement are often the key to innovation and creativity. The fifth-century BC Greek Philosopher Zeno of Elea was probably the first to underline the importance of dialectic in the search for truth. A century and a half later, the Chinese philosopher Zou Yan described how completeness can be achieved only by reuniting yin and yang, that is by associating the contradictory forces present in all things. But they were philosophers, and for mere mortals the idea that being disagreed with can have positive results is much more difficult to accept. In design as well as in any other collective enterprise, this very difficulty defines the mission of a leader: for the members of the team (and the leader themself) to agree that contradiction is legitimate, provided it is focused on the wish to achieve a result, and not on the people themselves. A dissenter is not necessarily an opponent, in contrast to what political (or corporate) life can lead one to think. Edsel Ford managed to convince his father that the Ford Model A had to be attractive, and later that an affordable V8 engine was the way to go. By doing so, he probably saved Ford. But, by listening to his son, so did Henry.

50

The School for the Future

The classical Greek poet, dramatist and philosopher Aristophanes is credited with the suggestion that education should be seen not as a process of filling up a vessel, but rather as one of lighting a fire. And I have to confess that throughout my life I have been a serial pyromaniac. Teaching has always fascinated me and I have always sought the company of those who struggle to learn, regardless of whether they are young or slightly less young, encouraging them through passion and conviction. What can be more inspiring than helping someone who wants to get on – to broaden their knowledge, to satisfy their curiosity and to progress? I have always believed that the urge to pass on one's expertise and share one's understanding is perhaps linked to an unacknowledged desire for immortality.

London's Royal College of Art, which opened its faculty for Vehicle Design in the 1970s, was host to my first role as an associate tutor. Later, when I was in charge of Renault Design, I lent my support to the founders of France's Strate School of Design as they established – at long last! – a department of Automobile Design; this quickly became a global benchmark thanks to the high quality of its teaching. Then in 1998 I was appointed chair of the board of directors of the École Nationale Supérieure de Création Industrielle (ENSCI), France's national school of industrial design. This highly innovative school was set up in the early 1980s, and my term of office was renewed three times.

Though I strongly welcomed this excellent pedagogical initiative and the high calibre of the staff and students, towards the end of my term of chairmanship I witnessed hostility between the two government ministries supporting the school. The ministries of culture and industry each wanted to place their own person in charge – one ministry felt that an artist should lead the organization, the other desired to promote the cause of genuine industrial design. In spite of pressure from the culture ministry's representative for the fine

arts it was Alain Cadix, an engineer of great renown, who was appointed chair of ENSCI in 2007. As the principal person promoting his candidacy I had to face a lot of acrimony in the lead-up to my departure at the end of my tenure. But the incoming chair of the school was able to implement a profound and welcome shift towards a more open attitude to design, one that tackled real issues – something that helped the school avoid sinking back into being a mere training ground for 'designer-decorators' producing high-society furniture, often uncomfortable and offered only within a closed circle of elite customers a million miles away from the ordinary consumer.

In 2011, just as I was embarking on my new life as a naval designer, I became involved in the setting up of a project at Strate to design a sailing yacht; this brought me back in touch with Maurille Larivière, one of the three founders of this excellent school and someone I had a lot of contact with while I was head of Renault Design. Maurille is a great sailing enthusiast and it turned out that he was also close to Marc Van Peteghem, one of the two principals of the renowned naval architecture firm VPLP, with whom I had struck up a close collaboration. Although we met up to talk boats and design, the conversation very quickly turned to the subject of education, and we all homed in on the idea that we needed to pioneer what we called 'a school for afterwards'.

All three of us believed strongly that we could no longer keep turning a deaf ear to what the scientists were saying and, in particular, to what the Israeli historian Yuval Noah Harari put forward in his international best-seller, *Homo Deus: A Brief History of Tomorrow* (2016), about the transformations that the human race is set to experience in the years to come. What will we become, and what will our future be? The topic is both edifying and terrifying. One of Harari's pivotal arguments is that within the space of a century our impact as humans could be even greater than that of the asteroid that killed off the

Left to right:
Patrick le Quément,
Maurille Larivière
and Marc Van
Peteghem.

dinosaurs some 65 million years ago. It was clear to the three of us that we could no longer remain passive onlookers: we needed to use our skills and make our own contribution by setting up the school for the future.

So it was with this in mind that we put together the framework for a project, which we then presented to a series of potential partners. We received especially enthusiastic support in Nice, and that is where we established our school in 2013, after three years of exploration, discussion and late-night debate.

Under the banner of The Sustainable Design School our international college is single-minded in its purpose, to foster sustainable design in the service of humanity. The school's five-year course is structured around a central core: building up understanding of sustainable development, and the application of eco innovation as well as frugal innovation. The school also teaches all the other skills that are part and parcel of a training in industrial design, such as drawing techniques and expertise with design software, as well as exploring the advent of new methods of creative thinking such as collective drawing, biomimicry and something that as a group we named 'the design of knowledge'. And of course our programme includes the teaching of functionality and the aesthetics of the object or service.

All the students are given the opportunity to take part in projects in partnership with major companies, organizations or NGOs, allowing them to build up real-life experience on actual schemes.

Buckminster Fuller, the visionary American ecologist, architect and designer, predicted as early as the 1960s that we would have to find different ways of managing our planet if humanity was to survive. A strong advocate of rigorous functionalism, he declared that 'Design stands between two poles: on the one side is utopia, and on the other is oblivion, which could become reality if designers remain preoccupied with trivial and purely aesthetic issues. But design could help promote utopia if it directed its creativity towards helping resolve the immense societal challenges of our age, the most pressing of which is the global warming that is threatening us.' It is imperative for everyone to become involved in shaping the radical changes in the global economy, in our behaviour and in our priorities – changes that are necessary to avoid the catastrophe that we know is around the corner.

At the Sustainable Design School we have made the choice to strive for the utopian solution, all the while keeping our feet firmly on the ground – something that, mercifully, has not prevented our project from taking off.

The little man in the street

There are two kinds of school: the ones where knowledge becomes faith, and is taken as an absolute truth; and the ones that are fuelled, not by absolute respect of tradition, but by the desire to improve on that tradition and to push it further. New Orleans jazz, as it is still played today in the Vieux Carré French quarter, is an example of the former: it brings to life what was, but does not give life to anything. Thankfully, musicians from Duke Ellington to John Coltrane and many others since used it as a starting point to reach new boundaries, and jazz as a whole is alive and well. Design today is at a crossroads, probably as much as it was when it was born in the late nineteenth century: are old shapes an absolute truth, or just the beginning of something to come? What will define a car in twenty years' time? What will mobility mean? Eventually, what will humans need? As the Finnish architect Alvar Aalto wrote in 1970, 'We should work for simple, good, undecorated things, but things which are in harmony with the human being and organically suited to the little man in the street.'

Epilogue

Fifty years in design – already! It all began with the subject I had chosen for my degree project, which involved science fiction, the first manned space missions of the 1960s, and a cyborg – a type of humanoid robot that anticipated the current concept of the enhanced or augmented human. What followed was an abrupt return to earth, as my first task as a professional car designer was to design a wheel trim for the Simca 1200S. After that came a large volume of automotive design work, then design director jobs at several automakers, the most demanding and the most impassioned of which was my role with Renault. It has all added up to an involvement with some sixty million vehicles, manufactured on several continents.

After I left my career in automotive design, I was lucky enough to be able to refocus my passion, seamlessly, onto sailing yachts. In parallel, I have been involved in founding a 'school for the future', the Sustainable Design School, based in Nice on the French Mediterranean coast and which opened its doors in 2013. Our graduates are already active in organizations and in civil society, where they are able to disseminate our shared values using the great sensitivity that they have developed...

I will end with the title of a song by Simon and Garfunkel, 'Still Crazy After All These Years'. Well, after so many years I am still just as crazy as ever about life, about the creative process, and also about communicating to others my life's experience – and I still believe, now more than ever, that where there is a will, there is a way.

Further Reading

DESIGN & AESTHETICS

Stephen Bayley, Terence Conran, *Design: Intelligence Made Visible* (Conran Octopus, 2007)

Henry Dreyfuss, *Designing for People* (Simon and Schuster, 1955)

Le Corbusier, *When the Cathedrals Were White* (Routledge, 1948)

Victor Papanek, *Design for the Real World: Human Ecology and Social Change* (Thames and Hudson, 1985, 2nd edition)

Nikolaus Pevsner, *Pioneers of Modern Design: From William Morris to Walter Gropius* (Penguin, 1960)

Junichiro Tanizaki, *In Praise of Shadows*, transl Thomas J Harper and Edward G Seidensticker (Leete's Island Books, 1977)

Hans M Wingler, *The Bauhaus: Weimar, Dessau, Berlin, Chicago* (MIT Press, 1978, 3rd edition)

CARS & CAR DESIGN

Serge Bellu, *Art de la carrosserie française: Du style au design* (ETAI, 2007)

Philippe Ladure, Philipp Moch, Pierre Vanier, Reg Winstone, *Voisin: La différence* (EPA Editions, 2014)

Michael Lamm, Dave Holls, *A Century of Automotive Style* (Lamm-Morada, 1996)

Tony Lewin, Ryan Borroff, *How to Design Cars Like a Pro* (Motorbooks, 2010)

Tom Wolfe, *The Kandy-Kolored Tangerine-Flake Streamline Baby* (Farrar, Straus and Giroux, 1965)

Michel Zumbrunn, Robert Cumberford, *Auto Legends: Classics of Style and Design* (Merrell, 2006)

CREATIVE STRATEGIES & MANAGEMENT TECHNIQUES

Kenneth Blanchard, Spencer Johnson, *The One Minute Manager* (William Morrow, 1982)

William Edwards Deming, *Out of the Crisis* (MIT Press, 1982)

Tom Kelley, *The Art of Innovation* (Broadway Business, 2001)

Tom Peters, Robert H Waterman, *In Search of Excellence* (Harper and Row, 1982)

Arthur P Sloan, *My Years at General Motors* (Doubleday, 1964)

James P Womack, Daniel T Jones, Daniel Roos, *The Machine That Changed the World* (Harper Perennial, 1991)

BIOGRAPHIES OF PATRICK LE QUÉMENT

Serge Bellu, *From Ford to Renault: 40 Years of Design, in the Footsteps of Patrick le Quément* (ETAI, 2011)

George Mason, *Patrick le Quément - Renault Design* (Automobilia Car Men, 2000)

Acknowledgements

Where should I start? From when should I begin? Should I thank once again my father, Jean le Quément, for having fallen for an English lady, who was at the time a nanny in a well-to-do aristocratic home and looked after the children of the deceased wife? For when my father passed away after a freak automobile accident, my mother sent me to school across the Channel in England, where I learned what resilience meant and how to practise what is known as being poker-faced. And so I began life unusually well groomed for what was to unfold before me.

I will not itemize my thanks through the decades that I lived wholeheartedly working as a designer in so many countries, meeting so many extraordinary individuals. I feel thankful for that experience, for those who shared their knowledge and became close friends, such as Antony Grade with whom I worked at Renault for so many years; and Serge Van Hove and Pascale Bauer, who were both at different times my executive secretaries. They all three helped me by giving me their creative comments. I would also like to express my gratitude to my sponsors Autodesk, SAE China Design Group, François Neveux and Ian Cartabiano, as well as to all those who placed pre-orders for this book: Autobest, Ian Cartabiano, Antony Grade, André Hefti, Lagoon Yachting, Nick Mason, François Neveux and VPLP Design, whose generosity made it possible to publish this book. Finally, thank you to all of you with whom I battled and who made my life sometimes so difficult; I will give no names for you were so many, but I still thank you for you made me want to write this book.

And then there are those who took part directly in the composition of *Design: Between the Lines*: Gernot Bracht, the talented, atypical designer who did the remarkable illustrations; and Stéphane Geffray, whose complementary texts offer a different viewpoint, as if entering a room you know well by climbing through the window. I would also like to thank my dear friend Jean-Marie Souquet, who gave me precious advice throughout the writing.

Tony Lewin translated my texts into English, as for some inexplicable reason I decided to write my perspectives in French when in reality I am more at ease writing in English; but then, Tony's result is perfectly in tune with the spirit of what I wrote, and it also respects my caustic sense of humour. What's more, Tony's knowledge of the French language, automobile history and design turned out to be invaluable.

This book of fifty perspectives could not have come to life were it not for the support and encouragement of Hugh Merrell, the publisher of *Design: Between the Lines*. I am also most grateful to have worked with Marion Moisy, whose sensitive editing and meticulous attention to detail have been so impressive throughout. And I would like to thank designer Nicola Bailey for her creative talent and the convincing layout she came up with.

Finally, I want to express my gratitude to all of my family, who did not see me for many months and particularly during a long summer season. To them and to my wife, Monique, who was so supportive and patient, I give my profound thanks.

Sponsors

The following organizations and individuals have made this book possible through their generous contributions.

FRANÇOIS NEVEUX

IAN CARTABIANO

AUTODESK makes software for people who make things. If you've ever driven a high-performance car, admired a towering skyscraper, used a smartphone or watched a great film, chances are you've experienced what millions of Autodesk customers are doing with our software. Autodesk gives you the power to make anything.

SAE CHINA DESIGN GROUP is a non-profit social organization founded by Chinese car-design professionals, dedicated to promoting Chinese car design and to working with international counterparts in order to enhance communication, prosperity and innovation.

216

Biographies

PATRICK LE QUÉMENT, a Frenchman who studied industrial design at the UK's Birmingham College of Art and Design in the 1960s, went on to become one of the most influential automobile designers of his era. His international career has taken in Simca, Ford, Volkswagen-Audi and Renault, where he was Senior Vice-President of Corporate Design. Since 2010 he has been active as a naval designer, and in 2013 he co-founded the Sustainable Design School, based in Nice on the French Riviera. Among the numerous awards he has received are European Designer of the Year and the Raymond Loewy Foundation's Lucky Strike Designer of the Year, both in 2002, and the EyesOn Design Lifetime Design Achievement award in 2015.

Patrick le Quément's texts were translated by **TONY LEWIN**, a journalist, author and translator based in Sussex, England, who has been writing about cars, car design and the automobile industry for decades. Among the books he has written are *The A-Z of 21st Century Cars* (2011), produced by Merrell, *The BMW Century* (2016) and *Speed Read: Car Design* (2017).

STÉPHANE GEFFRAY is a Paris-based writer, journalist and adjunct teacher at the Université de Paris Est-Créteil. His work regularly appears in the French editions of *Octane* and *Enzo* magazines. He also is a former editor of *Rétroviseur*, a leading French classic-car magazine. For this book, he wrote the texts accompanying Patrick le Quément's fifty perspectives.

GERNOT BRACHT is an automobile designer, illustrator and teacher of transport design and sketching techniques. Following a design career at various carmakers, including Renault in France, he now consults for several German automotive suppliers. He has taught at Germany's Hochschule Pforzheim design school since the early 2000s and also teaches at FH Joanneum University in Graz, Austria. He is the creator of all the illustrations featured in this book.

Index

Design: Between the Lines

First published 2019 by Merrell Publishers Limited, London and New York

Merrell Publishers Limited
70 Cowcross Street
London EC1M 6EJ

merrellpublishers.com

British Library Cataloguing in Publication data:
A catalogue record for this book is available from the British Library.

ISBN 978-1-8589-4676-4

Produced by Merrell Publishers Limited
Designed by Nicola Bailey
Edited by Marion Moisy
Proofread by Victoria Richards
Indexed by Hilary Bird

Printed and bound in China